DO-IT-YOURSELF GUIDES

Practical Projects
for the Home

Quality tools to build your world.

ACKNOWLEDGEMENTS

Created by Creative Publishing international
in conjunction with WSP Marketing International Ltd.,
47 Valleybrook Drive, Don Mills, Ontario M3B 2S6,
Canada.

**Creative Publishing International
Book Development Staff**

Vikki Anderson
Shawn Binkowski
Steve Boman
Janice Cauley
Marcia Chambers
Maren Christensen
Paul Currie
Doug Deutscher
Melissa Erickson
Jacque Fletcher
John Fletcher
Brad Kissell
Janet Lawrence
Bill Nelson
Chuck Nields
Jon Simpson
Greg Wallace
Gina Wornson

Printed on Canadian paper by World Color
Book Services, USA.

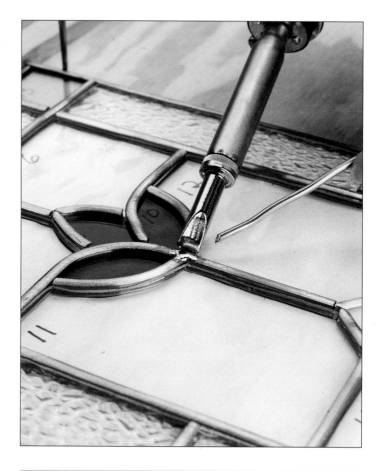

ISBN 0-86573-764-9

This book provides useful instructions but
we cannot anticipate all of your working
conditions or the characteristics of your
materials and tools. For safety, you should
use caution, care and good judgement
when following the procedures described
in this book. Consider your own skill level
and the instructions and safety precautions
associated with the various tools and
materials shown.

Creative Publishing international, WSP
Marketing International Ltd., Canadian Tire
Corporation, Limited or the Canadian Tire
Associate Dealers do not assume any
responsibility for damage to property
or injury to persons as a result of the use
of the information contained in this book.

Before commencing any project, consult
your local Building Department for information on building permits, codes and
other laws, as they may apply to your
project.

INTRODUCTION

Of the many delights in making a house a home, one of the most pleasing is finding the exact furnishing that provides you with that perfect sense of comfort, function or visual appeal. This is true whether you need an accent piece for the den or living room, an accessory for the kitchen or dining room, or something that solves a storage problem. And what better way to accomplish this than to create it yourself: you get exactly the piece you want and save money, too. *Practical Projects for the Home* contains plans for eleven projects that will improve and beautify your home.

Each project is demonstrated with detailed, step-by-step instructions and full-colour photographs. You'll also see the specific tools each project requires, as well as a materials list, a cutting list, and a construction diagram. You'll even find tips about tool use and finishing options.

You'll have a wonderful time creating these great designs – and you'll delight in how much money you save. Welcome to the world of Mastercraft Do-It-Yourself Guides!

TABLE OF CONTENTS

TOOL LIBRARY

To successfully make the projects seen in this book you need the proper tools, and they are shown here (except for the specialty tools required for stained glass work; they are shown on page 32). Quality tools, like Mastercraft, will serve your needs well. Keep hand tools protected and organized by storing them in a toolbox. Shelves or cabinets are good locations for power tools and supplies.

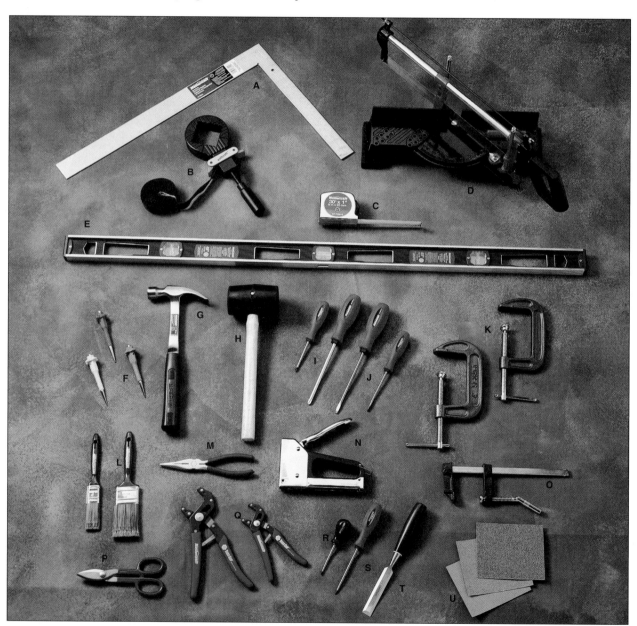

Basic hand tools: *carpenter's square (A), band clamp (B), tape measure (C), hand mitre box with saw (D), level (E), nail sets (F), hammer (G), mallet (H), Phillips screwdrivers (I), slot screwdrivers (J), C-clamps (K), brushes (L) needlenose pliers (M), staple gun (N), bar clamp (O), aviator snips (P), Robo-Grip® pliers (Q), awl (R), square drive screwdriver (S), chisel (T), sandpaper (U).*

Power tools: *router with router table (A), belt sander (B), power mitre saw (C), palm sander (D), circular saw (E), glue gun (F), drill (cordless or corded) (G), drum sanding attachment (H), spade bit (I), countersink bit (J), screwdriver bit (K), jigsaw (L).*

BOOKCASE

This classic tall bookcase is both attractive and functional, and it is simple to build.

The simple lines of this bookcase are given a more formal look by attaching trim moulding to the horizontal edges. The trim pieces on the shelves also provide more structural support. If you want to stain the bookcase to match other furniture, build it out of oak or pine materials.

Directions: Bookcase

1 Make the sides & front rail. The bookcase sides and the front rail have arches cut into their bottom edges to create the bookcase "feet."

A. Cut sides **(A)** and front rail **(C)** to size from 3/4"-thick plywood (we used birch).

B. Sand the parts smooth.

C. Clean the edges thoroughly, then cut strips of 3/4" self-adhesive veneer tape slightly longer than the long edges of each side.

D. Attach the tape by positioning it over one long edge of each side, then pressing it with a household iron set at a medium-low setting. The heat will activate the adhesive.

E. Sand the edges and surfaces of the taped edges to smooth out any rough spots.

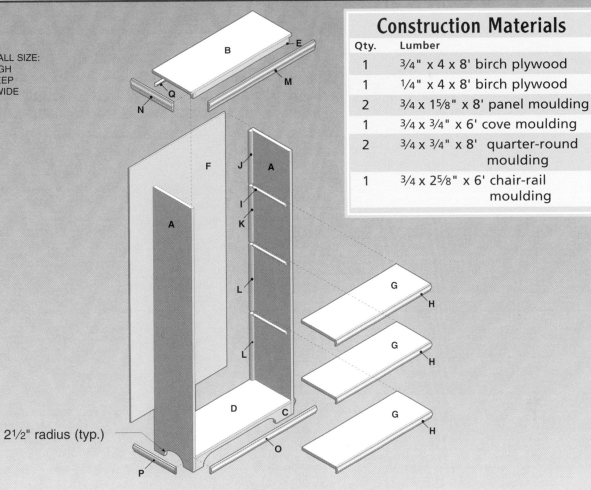

OVERALL SIZE:
72" HIGH
12" DEEP
31½" WIDE

2½" radius (typ.)

Construction Materials

Qty.	Lumber
1	¾" x 4 x 8' birch plywood
1	¼" x 4 x 8' birch plywood
2	¾ x 1⅝" x 8' panel moulding
1	¾ x ¾" x 6' cove moulding
2	¾ x ¾" x 8' quarter-round moulding
1	¾ x 2⅝" x 6' chair-rail moulding

Cutting List

Key	Part	Dimension	Pcs.	Material
A	Side	¾ x 12 x 71¼"	2	Plywood
B	Top	¾ x 11¾ x 31½"	1	Plywood
C	Front rail	¾ x 3¼ x 30"	1	Plywood
D	Bottom	¾ x 11¾ x 30"	1	Plywood
E	Top rail	¾ x 1½ x 30"	1	Plywood
F	Back	¼ x 30 x 68¾"	1	Plywood
G	Shelf	¾ x 10½ x 30"	3	Plywood
H	Shelf nosing	¾ x 1⅝ x 30"	3	Panel moulding
I	Shelf cleat	¾ x ¾ x 9¾"	6	Cove moulding
J	Back brace	¾ x ¾ x 14"	2	Quarter-round
K	Back brace	¾ x ¾ x 15"	2	Quarter-round
L	Back brace	¾ x ¾ x 18"	4	Quarter-round
M	Top facing	¾ x 2⅝ x 33"	1	Chair-rail moulding
N	Top side moulding	¾ x 2⅝ x 12¾"	2	Chair-rail moulding
O	Bottom facing	¾ x 1⅝ x 33"	1	Panel moulding
P	Bottom side moulding	¾ x 1⅝ x 12¾"	2	Panel moulding
Q	Back brace	¾ x ¾ x 28½"	1	Quarter-round

Note: Measurements reflect the actual thickness of dimensional lumber.
Materials: #6x2" wood screws, finish nails (4d, 6d), glue, 1¼" brad nails, ¾" wire nails, ¾" birch veneer edge tape (25'), sandpaper, putty, paint.

F. To make arches in the sides, designate a top and bottom to each side, and draw a cutting line across them, 2½" up from bottom edge. Draw marks on bottom edges of the sides, 5½" in from front and rear edges. Set a compass to draw a 2½"-radius arc, using marks on bottom edges as centrepoints: set the point of the compass as close to bottom edges of the sides as possible. Draw the arcs.

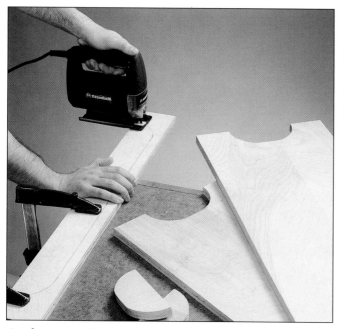

Arches cut along the bottoms of the side panels and front rail create the bookcase "feet."

G. Use a jigsaw to cut along the lines.
H. Repeat these steps to make the arch in the front rail, but place the point of the compass 4¾" in from each end of front rail.
I. Cut the front rail to shape with a jigsaw (photo above).

2 Build the carcass. The top, bottom and sides of the bookcase form the basic cabinet – called the carcass.
A. Cut the top **(B)**, bottom **(D)** and top rail **(E)** to size.
B. Sand parts to smooth out rough edges.
C. Draw reference lines across the faces of the sides, 3¼" up from the bottom edges.
D. Set sides on edge, and position bottom between them, just above reference lines.

E. Attach the bottom to the sides with glue and countersunk #6x2" wood screws, leaving a ¼" setback at the back edge.
F. Set the sides upright, and position the front rail between the sides, flush with the side and bottom edges.
G. Glue rail ends. Clamp to bottom board.
H. Drill pilot holes, and secure the front rail with 6d finish nails driven through the sides, and 1¼" brads driven through the bottom.
I. Set all nail heads below the wood surface.
J. Use glue and 6d finish nails to attach the top to the top ends of the sides, keeping the side and front edges flush.
K. Fasten the top rail between sides, flush with the front edges of the sides and top.
L. Use glue and 6d finish nails to secure the top rail in place.

3 Make the back. Quarter-round moulding is attached on sides and top to serve as retainer strips for ¼"-thick plywood back.
A. Cut the back braces **(J, K, L, Q)** to size from quarter-round moulding.
B. Set the carcass on its side.
C. Starting at the bottom, use glue and 1¼" brads to fasten back braces to sides and top, ¼" in from back edges (photo below).
D. Use a ¾"-thick spacer to create gaps for the shelves between the strips.
E. Position carcass so it rests on front edges.
F. Set the back in place so it rests on the back braces, and secure it with tape.

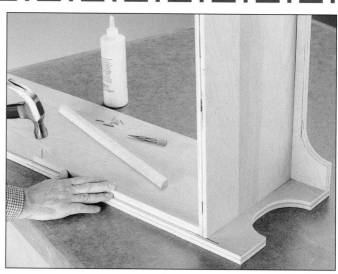

Attach the back braces to the sides, creating a ¼" recess for the back panel.

Strips of panel moulding are attached to the front edges of the shelves.

Attach the shelf cleats with glue and 1¼" brads.

G. Check for square by measuring diagonally from corner to corner across the back. When the measurements are the same, the carcass is square.

H. Drive ¾" wire nails through the back and into the back braces. Do not glue the back in place.

4 **Make the shelves.** Shelves are cut to size and inserted in the carcass between the back braces. Shelves are supported by shelf cleats.

A. Cut shelves **(G)** and shelf nosing **(H)** to size.

B. Drill pilot holes, and use glue and 4d finish nails to attach the nosing to the shelves, keeping the top edges flush (photo above left).

C. Set the nail heads.

D. Cut the shelf cleats **(I)** to size. To help you position the shelf cleats, use a combination square to draw reference lines square to the front edges of each side. Start the lines at the top of the lower back braces **(K, L)**, and extend them to within 1" of the front edges of the sides.

E. Apply glue to the shelf cleats, and position them on the reference lines.

F. Attach the shelf cleats to the inside faces of the sides with 1¼" brads (photo above right).

G. Apply glue to the top edges of the shelf cleats, then slide the shelves onto the cleats.

H. Drive 6d finish nails through the sides and into the ends of the shelves.

I. Drive ¾" wire nails through the back panel and into the rear edges of the shelves.

5 **Apply finishing touches.** Measure carefully and cut mouldings to fit your project.

A. Cut the top facing **(M)**, top side moulding **(N)**, bottom facing **(O)** and bottom side moulding **(P)** to size.

B. Mitre-cut both ends of top facing and bottom facing and front ends of side mouldings at a 45° angle so the moulding pieces will fit together at the corners.

C. Fasten the moulding at the top with glue and 4d finish nails, keeping the top edges flush with the bookcase.

D. Attach the bottom moulding, keeping the top edges flush with the bottom. To help you align the bottom side moulding, draw reference lines on the sides before attaching the pieces. The reference lines should be flush with the top of the bottom facing.

E. Attach the bottom side moulding.

F. Fill all holes with wood putty, and finish-sand the project.

G. Finish as desired – we used primer and two coats of interior enamel paint.

WINE CART

RECOMMENDED POWER TOOLS

MASTERCRAFT

CIRCULAR SAW

MASTERCRAFT

POWER DRILL

MASTERCRAFT

JIGSAW

MASTERCRAFT

PALM SANDER

• belt sander

RECOMMENDED HAND TOOLS

MASTERCRAFT

BASIC HAND TOOLS

• C-clamps
• carpenter's square

An elegant accessory for fine dining and entertaining, this solid oak wine cart with its lift-off serving tray is also very practical.

Beauty and function combine in this attractive design. It provides a clever transportable serving island for entertaining that is also a stunning display cabinet for bottle and stemware when not in use. The bottle racks are angled forward to keep the wine corks from drying out.

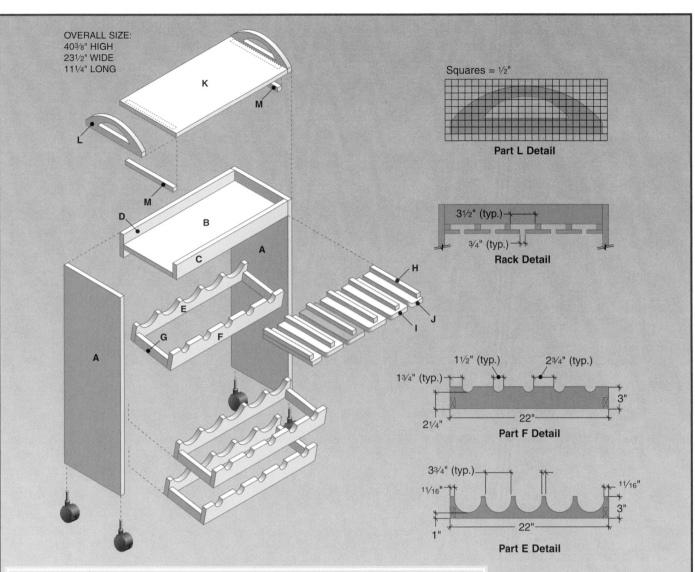

OVERALL SIZE:
40⅜" HIGH
23½" WIDE
11¼" LONG

Squares = ½"

Part L Detail

3½" (typ.)
¾" (typ.)

Rack Detail

1½" (typ.) 2¾" (typ.)
1¾" (typ.)
3"
2¼" 22"

Part F Detail

3¾" (typ.)
11/16"
11/16"
3"
1" 22"

Part E Detail

Cutting List

Key	Part	Dimension	Pcs.	Material
A	Side	¾ x 11¼ x 34"	2	Oak
B	Top	¾ x 9¾ x 22"	1	Oak
C	Front stretcher	¾ x 2½ x 22"	1	Oak
D	Back stretcher	¾ x 4 x 22"	1	Oak
E	Wine rack, back	¾ x 3 x 22"	3	Oak
F	Wine rack, front	¾ x 3 x 22"	3	Oak
G	Wine rack, cleat	¾ x 1½ x 6½"	6	Oak
H	Stemware slat	¾ x ¾ x 9¼"	6	Oak
I	Stemware plate	½ x 3½ x 9¾"	4	Oak
J	End plate	½ x 2⅛ x 9¾"	2	Oak
K	Tray	¾ x 11¼ x 22"	1	Oak
L	Tray handle	¾ x 3½ x 11¼"	2	Oak
M	Tray feet	¾ x ¾ x 9½"	2	Oak

Note: Measurements reflect the actual thickness of dimensional lumber.
Materials: Wood glue, #6 wood screws (1", 1¼"), casters (4), sandpaper, stain, polyurethane.

Construction Materials

Qty.	Lumber
2	1x12" x 6' oak
1	1x4" x 8' oak
1	1x4" x 6' oak
1	1x2" x 4' oak
1	½x2¾" x 2' oak
1	½x3¾" x 4' oak

Directions: Wine Cart

Use a spacer to keep the slats aligned properly, and attach with glue and countersunk screws.

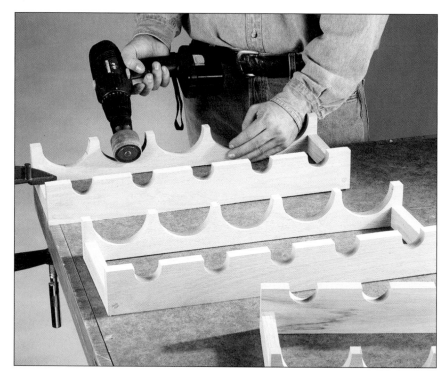

Use a drum sander attached to your portable drill to smooth the curved jigsaw cuts on each rack.

1 Construct the sides and stemware rack assembly. These form the basic structure of the cart.

A. Start by cutting the cart sides **(A)**, top **(B)** and back stretcher **(D)** from 1x12 oak.

B. Cut the front stretcher **(C)** from 1x3 oak and stemware slats **(H)** from 1x4 oak.

C. Cut the plates **(I)** and end plates **(J)** to size from 1/2"-thick oak.

D. Clamp a belt sander perpendicular to your worksurface, and round over the front corners of the stemware plates, as well as one corner of each end plate. A Mastercraft belt/disc sander will also do this well.

E. Sand the remaining cut edges smooth with a palm sander.

F. Next, position the top face-down, and arrange the slats on the top, flush against the back edge and evenly spaced 3½" apart (use a piece of scrap wood as a spacer). Keep the outer slats flush with the edges of the top.

G. Drill countersunk pilot holes and attach the cleats to the underside of the top piece with glue and 1¼" screws (photo above left).

2 Cut and assemble the wine racks. The wine racks are

TIP:

To check for squareness, measure your project from one corner diagonally to its opposite corner. Repeat the procedure for the other two corners. If the two diagonal lines are equal, your construction is square.

first assembled as individual units, and are then attached to the sides of the cart.

A. Cut the wine rack backs **(E)** and fronts **(F)** from 1x4 oak.

B. Cut the cleats **(G)** from 1x2 oak.

C. Transfer the pattern for the wine rack backs and fronts to each piece (see diagram page 15) and cut them out carefully with a jigsaw.

D. Position the cleats between the fronts and backs of the wine racks, and drill two counterbored pilot holes through the fronts and backs and into the ends of the cleats at each corner.

E. Join the pieces with glue and 1¼" screws, checking to make sure the wine racks are square.

F. Plug the counterbores with glued wood plugs.

G. Clamp each completed rack to your worksurface, and sand the curves smooth with a drum sander (photo opposite page bottom).

H. Use a palm sander to smooth the plugs, and any other rough edges.

3 **Attach the wine racks to the cart.** The racks are installed at a slight angle, to ensure that the wine in each bottle will be in constant contact with the cork. This keeps the corks moist and helps prevent them from cracking and spoiling the wine.

A. On the inside face of each side piece, measure up ½" from the bottom and make a mark along the front edge (photo below).

Clamp a 4x10" spacer *between the bottom and middle rack for proper position. Repeat for top rack.*

B. Measure up 2½" from the bottom and make a mark along the back edge.

C. Draw an angled reference line between the marks.

D. With one of the side pieces lying flat on your worksurface, position the first wine rack so the bottom edge is flush against the reference line and the front edge is set back ¾" from the front edge of the side piece.

E. Drill countersunk pilot holes and attach the rack to the side with glue and 1¼" screws.

F. Attach the middle rack and top rack in the same manner, using a 4x10" spacer to position them correctly (photo above).

G. Using bar clamps, position the opposite side piece, and arrange the stretchers in place between the sides.

H. Check to make sure the unattached cleats are at the proper position and that the stretchers are flush with the top edges of the cabinet.

I. Drill counterbored pilot holes, then use glue and 1¼" screws to anchor the stretchers and remaining cleats. **NOTE:** Check frequently during assembly to make sure the cabinet is square.

Measure ½" along front *and 2" along back of each side, and connect marks for bottom rack alignment.*

For consistent placement of the stemware racks, use a ³/₄" spacer to position the bottom plates on the slats.

4 Attach the top assembly. This provides stability and a place for the tray to sit.

A. Lay the cart on its side, and clamp the top between the side pieces. The bottom face of the top should be flush with the bottom edge of the front stretcher.

B. Drill three evenly spaced horizontal pilot holes through the outer slats into the sides, then use glue and screws to fasten the top to the sides from inside the cart.

C. Drill three evenly spaced counterbored pilot holes through the stretchers into the edges of the top, and secure with glue and 1¼" screws.

D. Position the cabinet upside down.

E. Centre the stemware plates over the slats, with the square end flush against the back stretcher, then drill three evenly spaced counterbored pilot holes along the centre of each plate.

F. Attach the plates to the slats with glue and 1" screws (photo above).

G. Attach the end plates to the outside slats with glue and 1" screws driven through counterbored pilot holes.

H. While the cart is still upside down, drill holes into the bottom edges of the cart sides, and test-fit the casters (photo opposite page above left).

While the cart is upside down, *drill the bottom edges of the sides for casters.*

G. Attach the handles to the tray with glue and 1¼" screws.

H. Position the tray feet ⅛" in from the sides of the tray bottom and ⅞" from the front and back.

I. Drill counterbored pilot holes, then attach the feet with glue and 1" screws.

6 Apply the finishing touches. If you will be using the tray as a cutting board, make sure to use a non-toxic finish.

A. Glue ⅜" oak plugs into each counterbore, and sand the plugs flush.

B. Sand the entire cart to 150-grit smoothness, and finish with your choice of stain (we used a rustic oak), and a polyurethane topcoat.

C. When the finish is dry, install the casters on the bottom of the cart.

TIP:
Brushing on a thin coat of sanding sealer before you apply wood stain will help the wood absorb stain more evenly and can eliminate blotchy finishes. Sanding sealer is a clear product, usually applied with a brush. Check the product labels on all the finishing products you plan to apply to make sure they are compatible.

5 Make the tray. The wine cart tray is simply a flat oak board with handles attached to the sides and narrow feet attached below.

A. Cut the tray bottom **(K)** from 1x12 oak.

B. Cut the tray handle blanks **(L)** from 1x4 oak.

C. Cut the ¾x¾" feet **(M)**.

D. Mark the pattern for the handles on the blank (see diagram page 13).

E. Drill a starter hole on the inside portion of the handle, then use a jigsaw to cut along the pattern lines (photo right).

F. Position the tray between the handles, then drill three evenly spaced counterbored pilot holes through the edge of each handle.

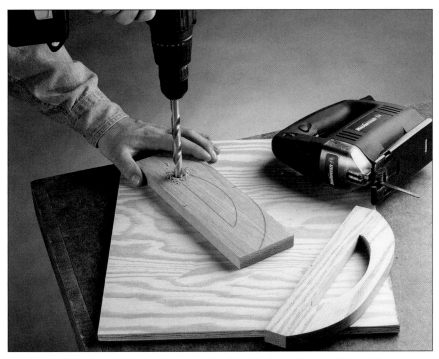

Drill a pilot hole *and then cut the inside handle profile with a jigsaw. Use scrap wood to support the workpiece and prevent tearouts.*

PIERCED METAL PANELS

Add a delightful country style to plain cabinets with these pierced metal panels.

Creating a comfortable country look is simply achieved by attaching these panels to cabinet doors. If the cabinet you wish to decorate has doors with recessed panels, mount the pierced metal panels in the recessed area. Some recessed panel doors have a removable centre panel that can be replaced with the metal panel. On a flat-surfaced door, create the panel look by mounting the pierced metal panel in the centre of the door, then trim the panel by edging it with narrow wood moulding. You will find instructions for both techniques in this project.

To make forming the metal panels easier, purchase pre-cut medium-gauge tin or copper sheets in sizes ranging from 5x7" to 12x18". You can easily trim them to your project's dimensions. Other metals that will work are thin-gauged galvanized sheet metal and hobby aluminum.

Metal piercing equipment is inexpensive. You can purchase the punching tools, awls and engravers at hardware stores in a variety of sizes.

TIP:
Before you begin your project, experiment on scrap metal to discover how hard to strike the piercing tools in order to create the desired effects. Practise until you are able to create holes that are consistent in size.

Directions: Pierced Metal Panels

1 **Making the pierced metal panel.**

A. Enlarge one of the designs (illustrations left) to project size. Cover with tracing paper, then copy the designs, using evenly spaced dots and dashes to indicate the holes and slits you choose to form the pattern.

B. Cut the metal to the correct size using aviator snips.

C. Remove fingerprints and smudges from the metal by rubbing it with fine steel wool.

D. Tape the metal along all edges to a piece of plywood, using wide duct tape.

E. Centre the pattern in the metal panel; tape in place (photo next page top).

F. Cushion the work surface under the plywood with several layers of newspaper.

G. Hold the piercing tool at a right angle to the metal surface, resting the point of the tool on a dot in the pattern.

H. Strike the tool with a mallet or hammer, driving the point through the metal.

I. Complete the entire pattern, using a larger tool on larger dots and a smaller tool on smaller dots.

Centre the tracing paper pattern *on the metal panel and tape in place.*

2 **Applying a pierced metal panel to a flat-surfaced door.** Make sure (by measuring the diagonals) that you cut the metal square.

A. Mark the desired outer dimensions for the moulding frame on the door, making sure the corners are squared.
B. Cut the metal with the length and width equal to these dimensions minus one width of moulding in each direction.
C. Pierce the metal panel with the desired pattern.
D. Measure and mark the length of the upper and lower moulding strips on the outer edge: mark the angle of the cut.
E. Cut the moulding strips, using a mitre box and backsaw.
F. Check to see that the moulding strips are exactly the same length.
G. Repeat to cut the side strips.
H. Paint or stain the moulding to match the wood in the door.
I. Mark the placement of the nail holes slightly towards the outer edge of the moulding

TIP:

You may purchase patterns for the pierced design. Or create your own pattern, using a simple line drawing or quilting stencil. Make a separate copy of the pattern for each panel you are piercing, saving the original. A new pattern is used for each panel so it is easy to see which holes have already been punched.

J. Use a chisel or engraver for dashes.
K. Remove the pattern slowly, checking that all holes and dashes are pierced.
L. Remove fingerprints and smudges with fine steel wool.
M. If you want to prevent the steel from aging, apply a coat of aerosol acrylic sealer. Or allow the metal to age naturally.

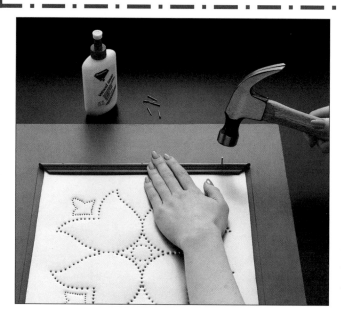

Carefully align *the upper moulding strip to the dimension marks in the door, making sure the strip overlaps the metal panel. Secure with brads driven through pre-drilled holes.*

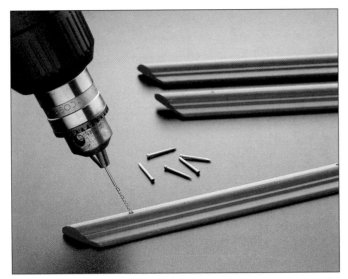

Use a drill and a bit slightly smaller than the brads to pre-drill the moulding.

strips, 1½" from the ends at the centre of each strip.

J. Pre-drill the nail holes, using drill bits slightly smaller than the brads you intend to use (photo above).

K. Centre the pierced metal panel on the door along marked lines for the frame. If the door is not lying horizontally, secure the metal pattern temporarily with masking tape.

L. Apply wood glue sparingly to the back of the upper moulding strip, towards the outer edge, using your finger.

M. Position the moulding strip on the door, aligning it with the markings and overlapping the upper edge of the metal panel (photo opposite page bottom); secure with brads, leaving the brads slightly raised.

N. Attach the moulding strips for the side of the panel, applying glue to the back and placing brads at the upper corners only.

O. Attach the lower strip making sure the frame is square. Secure the remaining brads for the sides of the frame.

P. Countersink the brads using a nail set. Touch up the nail holes and mitred corners with paint, or fill them with putty to match the stain.

Option: Applying a pierced metal panel to a recessed-panel door.

A. Cut the metal panels to the exact measurements of the recessed panel.

B. Pierce the metal.

C. Secure the metal inside the recess with small brads inserted at an angle; to prevent scratching, push the brads in place using a screwdriver covered with cloth (photo below).

D. Cut quarter-round or decorative moulding to fit the inside edge of the recess; use a mitre box to mitre the corners.

E. Paint or stain the moulding to match the door.

F. Mark the placement of the nail holes slightly towards the outer edge of the moulding strips, 1½" from the ends at the centre of each strip.

G. Pre-drill the nail holes using a bit slightly smaller than the brads you intend to use.

H. Apply wood glue sparingly to the back of the moulding strips, towards the outer edge, using your finger.

I. Position the moulding strips on the door, around the inner edge of the recessed area; nail in place leaving brads slightly raised.

J. Countersink the brads, using a nail set.

K. Touch up nail holes and mitred corners with paint, or fill them with putty to match the stain.

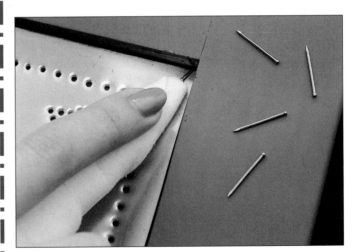

Use a screwdriver covered with cloth (to prevent scratching the metal) and push brads in to secure the panel.

CLOCKS

For Wood Clock

RECOMMENDED POWER TOOLS

JIGSAW

DRILL

RECOMMENDED HAND TOOLS

BASIC HAND TOOLS

- C-clamps
- nail set
- compass

NEEDED MATERIALS

- scraps of 1x2 lumber
- 1x8 board, for clock face
- 3" to 4" bezel clock insert
- wood glue
- 1½" brad nails
- paint or wood stain
- decorative handle or ornament, for top of clock

You can easily create your own custom clocks with decorative materials.

Battery-operated clock movements are available in a variety of sizes and styles that allow you to make your own clocks with wood left over from other projects or with decorative plates and frames.

Clock inserts come completely assembled and are simply placed into a round opening in the wood clock face. Springs hold the insert in place. Most inserts require a ¾" mounting depth.

Shaft-style clock movements are inserted from the back of the mounting surface through a small hole. The hands are then attached to the shaft. Several styles of hands are available with shaft-style movements. These movements can accommodate mounting depths up to ¾".

OVERALL SIZE:
11½" HIGH
9" WIDE
2" DEPTH

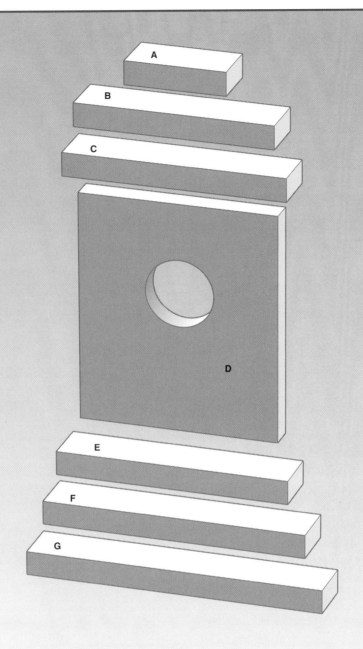

Cutting List

Key	Part	Dimension	Pcs.	Material
A	Top upper	¾ x 1½ x 3"	1	Pine
B	Top centre	¾ x 1½ x 6"	1	Pine
C	Top lower	¾ x 1½ x 6¾"	1	Pine
D	Clock face	¾ x 6 x 7"	1	Pine
E	Base upper	¾ x 1½ x 7"	1	Pine
F	Base centre	¾ x 1½ x 8"	1	Pine
G	Base lower	¾ x 1½ x 9"	1	Pine

Note: Measurements reflect the actual size of dimensional lumber.

Materials: wood glue, clock insert and mechanicals, sandpaper, paint or stain.

Directions: Mantel Clock

1 Make the clock face.

A. Cut one 6x7" wood piece for face of clock **(D)** from 1x8" board. Make sure to cut with grain of wood along length of piece.

Drill a starter hole for the jigsaw blade when cutting the hole for the clock.

B. Determine placement of clock insert.
C. Using a compass, mark diameter of back insert on wood at desired location.

2 Cut the clock insert hole.

A. Drill a ½"-dia. starter hole within the insert area.
B. Using a jigsaw, cut hole for clock just outside the marked line; this allows ease of inserting clock mechanism (photo above).
C. Check the fit of clock insert. Enlarge hole if necessary. Set aside clock insert.

3 Make the base and top of the clock.

A. Cut the base and top pieces.
B. Centre and glue bottom edge of clock face to top of 7" strip **(E)**; secure with 1½" brads.
C. Centre and glue 6¾" strip **(C)** to top edge of clock face; secure with brads, placing brads at least 1" from ends.
D. Centre and glue 8" **(F)** and 9" **(G)** base strips together; clamp and allow to dry (photo below).
E. Centre and glue 3" **(A)** and 6" **(B)** top strips together; clamp and allow to dry.
F. Glue base strips to bottom of clock case.
G. Glue top strips to top of clock case.
H. Paint or stain clock case as desired.
I. Attach clock insert; rotate to properly align dial.
J. Attach decorative piece to top of clock, if desired.

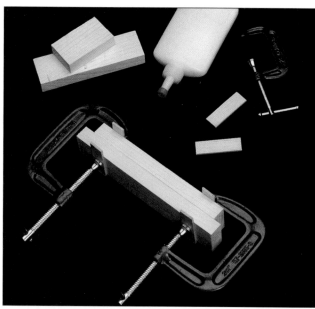

Use C-clamps to clamp the base pieces together after gluing. Note the use of scrap wood as clamp pads to prevent damage to surfaces.

For Plate/Frame Clock

RECOMMENDED POWER TOOLS

- glue gun

RECOMMENDED HAND TOOLS

NEEDED MATERIALS

- ceramic, glass plate or picture frame
- shaft-style battery-operated clock movement
- glass and tile drill bit
- mineral spirits for drilling glass or ceramic
- glue sticks
- wood glue
- wood stain or acrylic paints
- wooden ball
- brass or wooden ring
- acrylic sealer

Directions:
Plate or Frame Clock

Use hot glue to form a well holding mineral spirits when drilling the plate.

TIP:

Select the appropriate size Mastercraft glass and tile bit when drilling through glass and ceramics. Using a glass and tile bit will ensure that the glass or ceramic will not chip while drilling.

C. Insert shaft through plate; secure with brass washer and hex nut (photo below).

3 Attach clock face.

A. Attach hour hand; press lightly, taking care not to bend hand.
B. Attach minute hand. Secure hands with a cap nut or an open nut, then attach second hand.
C. Apply self-adhesive dial markings and numerals, if desired.

1 Drill the ceramic or glass plate.

A. Mark centre of plate for placement of clock shaft.
B. Pour mineral spirits into plate. For a flat plate surface, create a well by applying a ring of hot glue to the plate; fill the well with mineral spirits.
C. Drill hole the diameter of clock shaft, using a ceramic drill bit; drill slowly to minimize risk of breakage (photo above).
OPTION: Drill the picture frame.
A. Mount picture or decorative paper in frame.
B. Mark location of the hole for the clock shaft.
C. Drill hole the diameter of shaft, using the appropriate drill bit; drill slowly to minimize risk of cracking or tearing.

2 Insert clock mechanism.

A. Mount hanger, if desired, on shaft.
B. Place rubber gasket over the hole in the plate.

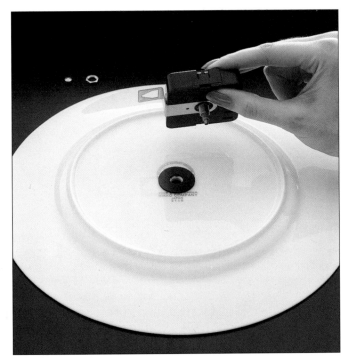

A rubber gasket protects the plate when attaching the shaft-style movement.

PICTURE FRAMES

MASTERCRAFT
CIRCULAR SAW

MASTERCRAFT
POWER DRILL

MASTERCRAFT
PALM SANDER

MASTERCRAFT
ROUTER

- power mitre saw or hand mitre box and saw
- belt sander or belt/disc sander

RECOMMENDED HAND TOOLS

MASTERCRAFT
BASIC HAND TOOLS

- band clamp
- router table

Create these classy frames to display the ones you love in style.

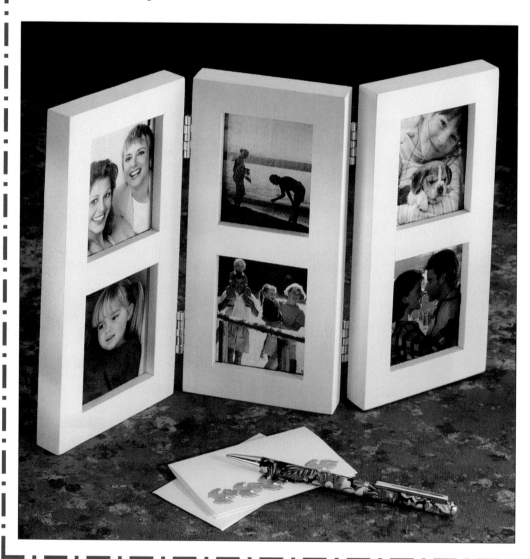

You can make these simple but attractive frames for your family pictures or as ideal gifts for friends and relatives. These plans can be easily modified to make frames that hold pictures of other sizes by proportionally adjusting the dimensions – just use the same construction methods. The design allows for the set of frames to be freestanding or you can hang it on a wall.

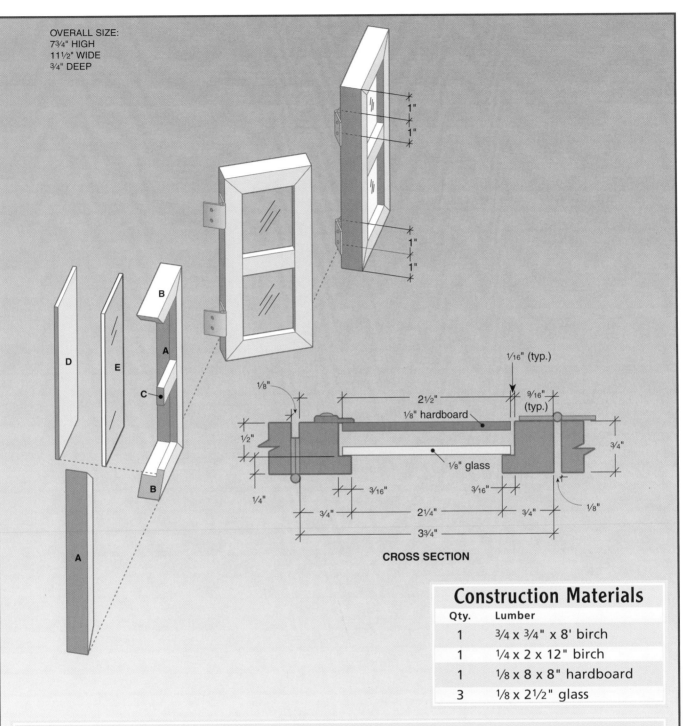

OVERALL SIZE:
7¾" HIGH
11½" WIDE
¾" DEEP

1"
1"
1"
1"

D
E
B
A
C
B
A

1/16" (typ.)

1/8"

2½"

1/8" hardboard

9/16"
(typ.)

½"

1/8" glass

3/4"

3/16"

3/16"

1/4"

3/4"

2¼"

3/4"

1/8"

3¾"

CROSS SECTION

Construction Materials

Qty.	Lumber
1	¾ x ¾" x 8' birch
1	¼ x 2 x 12" birch
1	1/8 x 8 x 8" hardboard
3	1/8 x 2½" glass

Cutting List

Key	Part	Dimension	Pcs.	Material
A	Frame side	¾ x ¾ x 7¾"	6	Birch
B	Frame top/bottom	¾ x ¾ x 3¾"	6	Birch
C	Mullion	¼ x ¾ x 2¼"	3	Birch
D	Backer	1/8 x 2½ x 6½"	3	Hardboard
E	Glass	1/8 x 2½ x 6½"	3	Glass

Note: Measurements reflect the actual thickness of dimensional lumber.
Materials: Wood glue, 4 brass hinges (1x½"), 12 retaining clips, sandpaper, paint or stain.

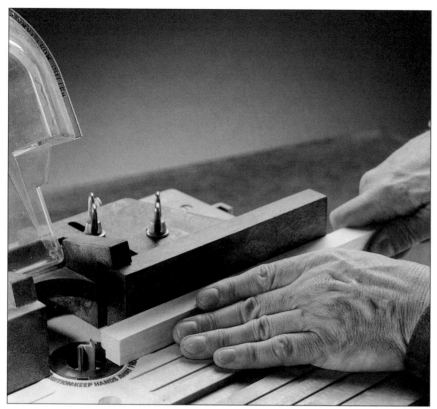

Use a router table and straight bit to cut the rabbets on the frame pieces.

Use a power mitre box to mitre-cut the frame pieces to length.

Directions: Picture Frame

1 Cut the parts. To cut the rabbets on the inside edges of the frame pieces, we recommend using a router table and a straight router bit. (You also can use a chisel, but this requires much more time and effort.) Make test cuts on scrap material to ensure accurate rabbets.

A. Set the fence of the router table to 3/16".

B. Cut the rabbets on the frame pieces by making multiple passes, gradually extending the depth of the cut until you achieve the 1/2" depth (photo above left). This technique creates a cleaner rabbet and reduces the risk of tearouts.

C. Using a power mitre saw (or hand mitre box and saw), carefully cut the frame sides **(A)** and tops/bottoms **(B)** to length, mitring the ends at 45° (photo above).

D. Clamp a stop block to the fence of the mitre saw to ensure the pieces are cut to the exact same length.

2 Assemble the frames. Take your time and make sure the frames are square.

A. Glue the frame sides, bottoms and tops together, and secure with band clamps (photo opposite page top).

B. Make sure the frames are square.

C. Leave excess glue until it hardens, then gently remove the dried glue with a sharp chisel.

D. Rip-cut 1/4" stock to 7/8" width, then cut the mullions **(C)** to length.

E. Mark a "sand-to" line on the mullions.

F. Clamp a belt sander onto your worksurface in a horizontal position, then grind down the mullions to the marked lines (photo below). You also can use a belt/disc sander if you have one.

G. Test-fit the mullions in the frames.

H. Attach with glue, and clamp until dry.

3 **Attach the hinges.** Align appropriately and clamp frame sections together to make accurate hinge installation easier.

A. Measure, mark and drill pilot holes for attaching the hinges but do not attach them yet.

B. Make sure you allow for the width of the hinge barrels when you align the frames for marking and drilling the pilot holes.

C. The hinges connecting the first and middle frames are attached to the frame sides and the hinges connecting the middle and last frames are attached to the back faces of the frames.

4 **Apply finishing touches.** If you want to highlight the wood grain, you can use an aniline dye to stain the wood, provided the joints are tight and clean. Otherwise, paint is always a good option.

A. Finish-sand the project.

B. Finish as desired.

C. After the finish dries, install the hinges.

D. Cut the hardboard backers **(D)** to size.

E. Insert the glass, photographs and backers.

F. Add a layer of cardboard as a spacer, then secure with retaining clips.

Join the frame pieces with glue and secure them with band clamps until the glue dries.

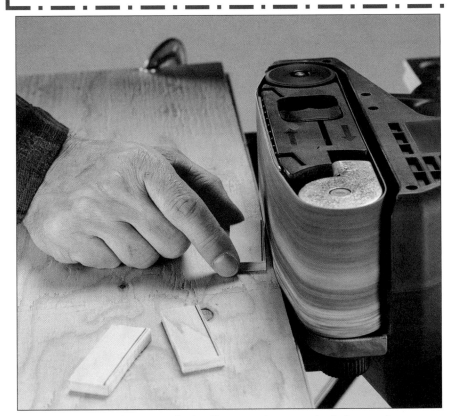

Use a belt sander or a belt/disc sander to grind down the mullions to the "sand-to" lines.

STAINED GLASS

Nothing captures beauty, artistry and light in quite the same way as stained glass.

We have designed a stained-glass project that will provide you with the basics of stained-glass construction, as well as a stylish finished project. Relevant skill building information follows each of the major project building sections. Read all of the skill building information before beginning to work.

It is important that you have the right tools and materials when you begin creating

stained glass. Stained-glass shops or some hobby shops will be able to provide you with the tools and materials necessary to complete this project. You also can find patterns for other stained-glass projects at these stores. Look in your phone book under Glass, Stained – Leaded, to find a store near you.

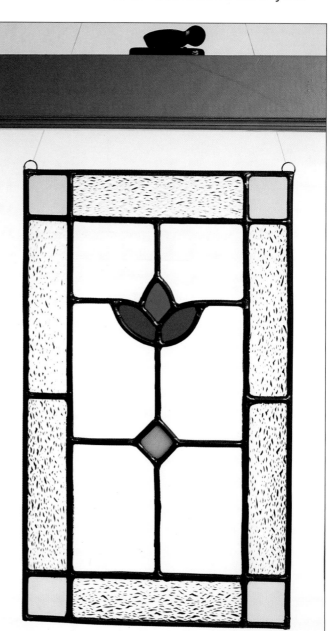

RECOMMENDED HAND TOOLS

MASTERCRAFT

BASIC HAND TOOLS

- diagonal pliers
- linesman pliers
- glazier's hammer (regular small hammer)

- utility knife
- scissors
- permanent marker
- glass cutter
- safety glasses
- carborundum stone
- wire brush
- 60 or 80 watt soldering iron
- flux brush
- scrub brush

NEEDED MATERIALS

- paper
- tag board
- masking tape
- glue stick
- glass per your pattern
- lead cames: H, 12'; U, 6'
- solder flux
- 60/40 solder
- grout
- ¾" brad nails

- sawdust or whiting powder
- small jar with cloth soaked in glass-cutting oil
- horseshoe nails
- lath strips
- skewer or sharp wooden dowel
- project board: 18 x 24" piece of ½" plywood
- spray glue

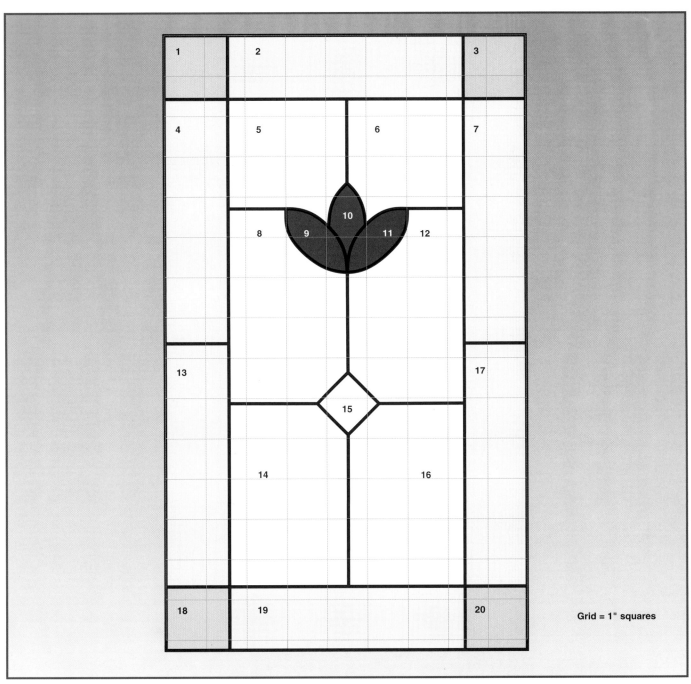

Cutting List

Piece #(s)	Dimension	Colour	Pcs.	Material
1, 3, 18, 20	1½ x 1½"	Green	4	Glass
2, 19	1½ x 5⅞"	Textured Clear	2	Glass
4, 7, 13, 17	1½ x 6"	Textured Clear	4	Glass
5, 6	2⅞ x 3"	Clear	2	Glass
8, 12	2⅞ x 4¾"	Clear	2	Glass
9, 11	1 x 2"	Red	2	Glass
10	1 x 1½"	Blue	1	Glass
14, 16	2⅞ x 4½"	Clear	2	Glass
15	1 x 1"	White	1	Glass

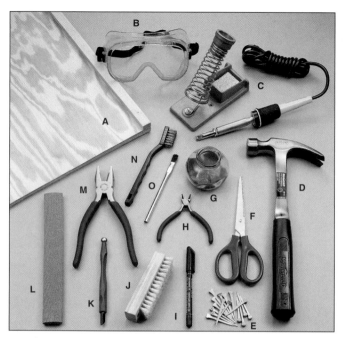

Tools and materials for stained-glass work:
project board with lathe (A), safety glasses (B), soldering iron and stand (C), hammer (D), horseshoe nails (E), scissors (F), small jar with oiled cloth (G), diagonal pliers (H), pen (I), scrub brush (J), glass cutter (K), carborundum stone (L), linesman pliers (M), wire brush (N), flux brush (O) tag board (P), carbon paper (Q), paper (R), pattern (S), U lead (T), H lead (U), solder flux (V), 40/60 solder (W), glass (X), grout (Y), glue stick (Z), sawdust (AA), masking tape (BB).

Directions: Stained Glass

1 Making the pattern and the template.

A. Make two full-size enlargements of the design. Use spray adhesive to mount one onto the tag board; this will be the template for cutting the glass pieces. The other will be the pattern.

B. Starting in the top left corner of the template and the pattern, number each piece.

C. Cut apart the template pieces. Trim the edges of each piece so that all of the black line is gone. This will allow for the space the heart (centre) of the lead pieces (called cames) will take up.

D. Place the template pieces on the pattern copy. Check to be sure that there is adequate space around each piece for the cames.

Skill Building: Pattern & Template Making

❑ The easiest way to enlarge a design to the necessary size for the pattern and the template is to use a photocopy machine. If you are unable to access a photocopy machine, draw a grid with 1" squares onto a piece of paper large enough for the pattern and onto the tag board. Using the grid as a guide, copy the design from page 31. Use carbon paper to make a duplicate copy.

❑ Place the template pieces on the glass so that lines and colour fluctuations in the glass run in the same direction once placed in the project.

❑ Glue the template pieces to the smooth side of the glass. Make sure there is enough space between the template pieces to make the necessary cuts, and yet not so much that you are wasting glass.

Blocking is the process of cutting large sheets of glass into smaller sections until each project piece stands alone.

Cutting the final shape of each piece is done with a series of cuts. You must score from edge to edge on the glass to make a successful break.

2 Cutting the glass.

A. Using a glass cutter, score straight lines from one edge to the other of the glass to cut the template pieces into sections (this is called blocking).

B. Break the glass into these large pieces using your hands and linesman pliers. Be sure to wear safety glasses when breaking glass.

C. Continue scoring with straight lines and breaking until each piece of the template is separated (photo above left).

D. Using the glass cutter, score the glass to the exact shape of the pattern piece (photo above right).

E. Trim away excess glass with the linesman pliers (this is called grozing). Practice this skill on scrap pieces of glass before you attempt it on pattern pieces. Apply light pressure with the pliers to nibble away small pieces of protruding glass (photo bottom right).

F. Use the carborundum stone to rub the edges of the glass, removing any excess glass or irregularities. Shape the glass to the pattern shape.

G. Leave the template in place on each piece until you are ready to position it when assembling.

Grozing removes as much excess glass as possible, making final smoothing with carborundum stone easier.

TIP:
Use linesman pliers for breaking and grozing. The large, square-tipped jaws are more effective than slip/combination style pliers. Diagonal pliers easily cut the lead cames to length.

Skill Building: Cutting Glass

❏ Cutting glass consists of two steps: scoring the glass with a glass cutter and breaking the glass using linesman pliers and your hands (photo right).

❏ Before you begin cutting the project pieces, use a scrap piece of glass to practise your cutting.

❏ Always score glass on a smooth, flat surface.

❏ Hold the glass cutter so that it is comfortable in your hand.

❏ Always score the glass from edge to edge.

❏ Push the cutter along the template piece, so that you can see where you are going.

❏ Use the proper pressure when scoring the line. If the pressure is too light, the glass will not break properly; if the pressure is too heavy, small fractures can form in the glass.

❏ Use even pressure and speed through the entire score.

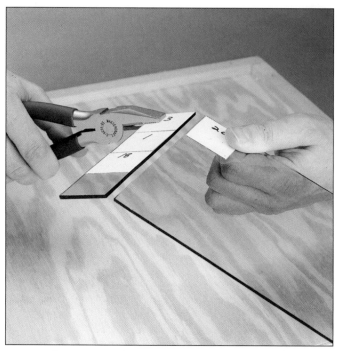

Use a downward snapping motion *to make a clean break after scoring.*

❏ Keep the cutting wheel perpendicular to the piece of glass.

❏ Lubricate the cutting wheel after each score with an oil-soaked rag.

❏ Breaking curves can be difficult when the curve is deep. When breaking curves, stained-glass artists will often score and make several straight breaks, making the curved break smaller and easier to manage.

❏ Break as much excess glass away as possible before scoring and breaking the curve (photo left).

❏ Score from one end of the curve to the other using constant pressure.

❏ Use pliers to break the curve. Start the break at one end of the score line and progress to the other. Trim away excess glass in the curve with the pliers so that the curve follows the pattern piece.

❏ Using the carborundum stone, shape the edges of the curve.

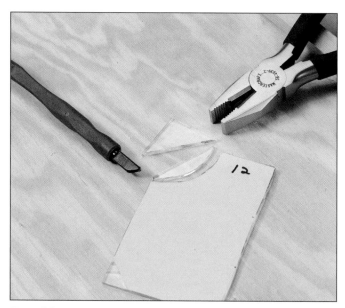

Breaking curves *is most successful when you remove as much excess glass as possible before scoring and breaking the curved portion.*

3 Assembling the glass with leading.

A. Tape the paper copy of the pattern to a project board. Line the top and left side of the pattern with wood lath, then attach the lath to the project board with brads.

B. Stretch the U came straight. Secure one end of it in a vise and pull it with a pair of pliers until it is straight.

C. Cut the top and left side piece of U came to length and place along the side and the top of the pattern.

D. Insert the first piece of glass in the upper left corner of the project. Be sure that the glass fits snugly into the U came, and that the free edges of the glass lie inside the lines for the piece in the pattern.

E. Hold a short length of H came up to the inside edge of piece 1; mark the lead a short distance (see Skill Building, right) from where the pattern lines intersect.

F. Cut the lead with diagonal pliers. Make sure that the H came is a little bit shorter than the pattern line to allow for the came that will meet it.

G. Add the second piece of glass and edge with the H came. Continue to add and edge until all of the pattern pieces have been inserted, using horseshoe nails to hold pieces in place as necessary (photo below).

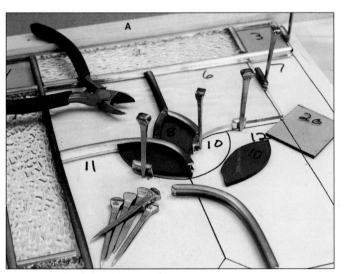

Horseshoe nails *and scrap lead pieces help keep the project in position as you work. Note the lath piece (A) used as a firm border while assembling the project.*

Skill Building: Leading

- ❑ Leading is not an exact science. Do not worry about making mistakes; they are easily correctable. With time and practice you will get comfortable with the necessary skills.
- ❑ U came (glass fits in one side only) is used for the border, H came (glass fits in both sides) for the interior of the project.
- ❑ Cames need to be a little shorter than the pattern lines to allow for the width of the connecting came (half the width for an H came and the whole width for a U came). If the came is a little too short, you can fill this gap when soldering.
- ❑ If the leading is much shorter than the pattern piece, a patch can be applied to fill the gap. To do this, cut a patch and solder it in place.
- ❑ Often when leading, the project tends to grow because the length of the lead is too long. Continually check the project against the pattern to make sure that your finished product is not too large.
- ❑ When you are fitting lead to curved pieces of glass, hold the glass in your hand and shape the lead around it.
- ❑ If the lead channels are not wide enough to fit the glass, widen them with a utility knife.
- ❑ Use horseshoe nails to temporarily hold glass and keep it firmly in position while you are assembling the project (photo left). Place a small piece of scrap lead between the glass and the nail, then tap the nail into the project board.

WARNING: Lead is a toxic substance. Both the cames and solder should be handled with care. Wash your hands often while working. Avoid contact with your mouth and face after handling lead, until you have thoroughly cleaned your hands. Work in a well-ventilated room when soldering. Make sure lead products are stored out of the reach of children.

TIP:

Make sure you use a soldering iron that is designed for stained-glass work. The more common soldering guns and irons used for soldering electrical connections have small, pointed tips that are not capable of properly melting and flowing the solder into the joints between cames.

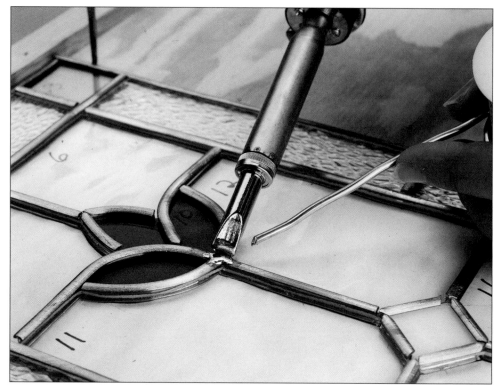

Soldering the joints *between the lead cames creates a rigid frame. Do not touch the tip of the soldering iron to the cames or the glass.*

4 Soldering the lead joints.

A. Use a wire brush to clean the lead joints to be soldered.

B. Apply flux paste to the joint with a flux brush.

C. Use a 700° F (371° C) soldering iron (60 or 80 watt) to solder the joints. Melt a ¼" section of the solder wire to the bottom of the iron, lower the iron to the joint and the solder will flow into the joint and bond the cames (photo above).

D. Solder all the joints on one side of the project.

E. Flip the project over, and solder all the joints on the other side of the project.

Skill Building: Soldering

❏ Soldering bonds the leading together with strong tight seams. It is important to solder joints well in order to maintain the structural integrity of the project. Practise on a couple of scrap pieces before you begin soldering your project.

❏ Apply flux to the joint before you begin soldering. Flux disperses heat and allows the solder to bond to the leading. Without flux it is nearly impossible to make a good joint.

❏ Wipe the tip of the hot iron occasionally on a damp rag or sponge. A clean tip helps disperse the heat better.

❏ Be careful to not overheat the leading, as the leading will melt. Also, if the glass heats up, it may crack. Let the solder flow into the joint; keep the soldering iron from contacting the project as much as possible.

❏ Flux and solder one joint at a time, working your way from left to right down the project.

5 Grouting and cleaning the panel.

A. Using your fingers, push the grout between the glass pieces and the flanges of the cames. Don't exert too much pressure on the project.

B. Use sawdust or whiting powder and a scrub brush to rub off excess grout and flux.

C. After removing grout and flux, brush off the sawdust or whiting powder. Remove any remaining sawdust or whiting powder and grout that the scrub brush did not remove with a skewer or sharp wooden dowel. Be careful to not gouge out grout from the flanges.

D. Turn the panel over and grout the other side.

E. If you notice oxidation occurring in the leading, rub it off with the wire brush. Buff the leading with a clean rag to darken the solder.

F. Allow the grout to set, then clean the project.

Grout the project, using your fingers to force grout into the space between the flanges and the glass.

Skill Building: Grouting

❑ Grouting fills the spaces between the glass and the lead, keeping the glass from rattling or becoming loose. Grouting is a messy job, but well worth the final result.

❑ Use liberal amounts of grout on your finger and push it into the lead channels (photo top right).

❑ Be sure to grout all of the lead pieces on both sides of the project.

❑ After you have finished grouting, clean the surface of excess grout using sawdust or whiting powder and a stiff scrub brush. Use a liberal amount of the cleaning material and cover the surface of the project (photo bottom right).

❑ Allow the grout to set for three days before wetting the surfaces to clean.

❑ After grout has set, clean both sides of the project in warm soapy water. Do not immerse the project or let it soak; the grout can soften and come out.

Remove excess grout with sawdust and a stiff brush.

MUSKOKA CHAIR

This delightful Muskoka chair provides classic style and comfort when you are relaxing outdoors.

The traditional Muskoka chair, with its simple, clean lines, is an attractive addition to any outdoor setting, whether on the patio, deck, porch or lawn. You will find it is an easy project to build and add to your outdoor lifestyle. If you want to paint your chair, build it out of pine and use a quality exterior gloss enamel paint. Otherwise, use cedar and coat the chair with a clear exterior wood sealer.

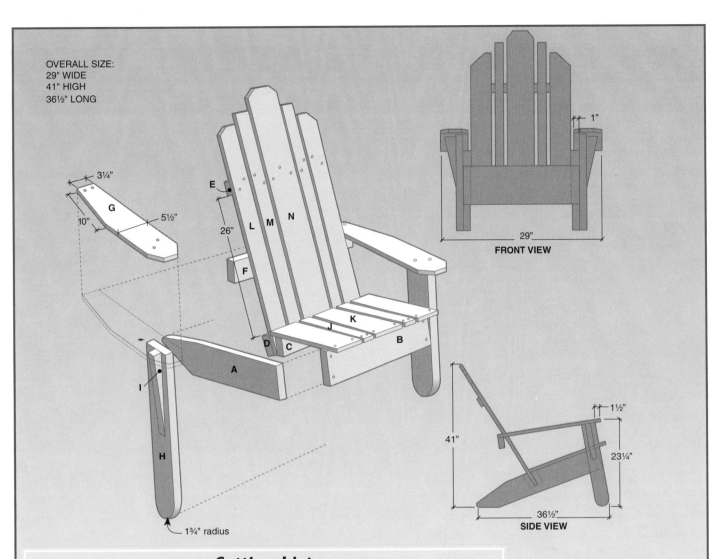

OVERALL SIZE:
29" WIDE
41" HIGH
36½" LONG

FRONT VIEW

SIDE VIEW

1¾" radius

Cutting List

Key	Part	Dimension	Pcs.	Material
A	Leg	1½ x 5½ x 34½"	2	Cedar
B	Front	1½ x 5½ x 21"	1	Cedar
C	Seat support	1½ x 3½ x 18"	1	Cedar
D	Low back brace	1½ x 3½ x 18"	1	Cedar
E	High back brace	¾ x 3½ x 18"	1	Cedar
F	Arm cleat	1½ x 3½ x 24"	1	Cedar
G	Arm	¾ x 5½ x 28"	2	Cedar
H	Post	1½ x 3½ x 22"	2	Cedar
I	Arm brace	1½ x 2¼ x 10"	2	Cedar
J	Narrow seat slat	¾ x 1½ x 20"	2	Cedar
K	Seat slats	¾ x 5½ x 20"	3	Cedar
L	End back slat	¾ x 3½ x 36"	2	Cedar
M	Narrow back slat	¾ x 1½ x 38"	2	Cedar
N	Centre back slat	¾ x 5½ x 40"	1	Cedar

Note: Measurements reflect the actual size of dimensional lumber.
Materials: Moisture-resistant glue, deck screws (1¼", 1½", 2", 3"), ⅜ x 2½"
lag screws with washers, sandpaper, paint or wood sealer.

Construction Materials

Qty.	Lumber
1	2x6" x 8' cedar
1	2x4" x 10' cedar
1	1x6" x 14' cedar
1	1x4" x 12' cedar
1	1x2" x 8' cedar

Directions: Muskoka Chair

1 Cut the legs. Wide, sprawling back legs that support the seat slats and stretch to the ground on a near-horizontal plane are telltale features of Muskoka-style chairs.

A. Cut two 34½"-long pieces of 2x6.

B. Mark the tapers onto the back end of one board by marking a point on the end of the board, 2" from the edge. Then mark another point on the edge, 6" from the end. Connect the points with a straightedge.

C. Mark another point on the same end, 2¼" in from the other edge. Mark a point on that edge, 10" from the end. Connect these points to make a cutting line for the other taper.

D. Make the two taper cuts with a circular saw.

E. Use the leg as a template for marking identical tapers on the other leg board. Cut the second leg (photo below).

Cut tapers into the back edges of the legs.

2 Build the seat. The legs form the sides of the box frame that supports the seat slats.

A. Cut the front apron (**B**) and seat support (**C**) to size.

B. Attach the apron to the front ends of the legs with glue and 3" deck screws driven through counterbored pilot holes.

C. For the 3" deck screws used throughout most of this project, drill ⅛"-dia. pilot holes through ⅜"-dia. x ¼"-deep counterbores, then insert ⅜"-dia. cedar plugs into the counterbores when assembly is finished.

D. Position the seat support so the inside face is 16½" from the inside edge of the front apron.

E. Attach the seat support between the legs, making sure the tops of the parts are flush.

F. Cut the seat slats (**J**) and (**K**) to length from the 1x2 and 1x6, respectively, and sand the ends smooth.

G. Arrange the slats on top of the seat box with ⅜" spaces between slats – use wood scraps as spacers. The slats should overhang the front of the seat box by 3/4".

H. Fasten the seat slats by driving counter-bored 2" deck screws through the ends of the slats and into the top of the front apron and the seat support in back. Be careful to keep the counterbores aligned so the cedar plugs form straight lines across the front and back of the seat.

I. Once all the slats are installed, use a router with a ¼" roundover bit (or a power sander) to smooth the edges and ends of the slats (photo below).

Round over the sharp slat edges *with a router or power sander.*

Make decorative cuts, using a jigsaw, on the fronts of the arms (shown) and the tops of the back slats.

3 **Make the back slats.** Like the seat slats, the back slats in our design are made from three sizes of dimensional lumber (1x4, 1x2 and 1x6).

A. Cut the back slats **(L)**, **(M)**, **(N)**, to size.

B. For a decorative touch that is simple to create, we trimmed off corners on the wider slats. On the 1x6 slat **(N)**, mark points 1" in from the outside top corners of the slat, then mark points on the outside edges, 1" down from the corners. Connect the points, then trim off the corners with a jigsaw, following the lines.

C. Mark the 1x4 slats **(M)** 2" from one top corner, in both directions. Draw cutting lines, then trim off the corners.

4 **Attach back slats to braces.** This will make the chair back unit.

A. Cut the low back brace **(D)** and high back brace **(E)**.

B. Set the braces on a flat worksurface, then slip ¾"-thick spacers under the high brace so the top is level with the low brace.

C. Arrange the back slats on top of the braces with the same pattern and spacing used with the seat slats. The untrimmed ends of the slats should be flush with the

bottom edge of the low back brace, and the bottom of the high back brace should be 26" above top of the low brace.

D. Use ¾" spacers to set gaps and make sure the braces are exactly perpendicular to the slats.

E. Attach the slats to the low brace with counterbored 2" deck screws, and to the high brace with 1¼" deck screws.

5 **Cut the arms.** The broad arms of this Muskoka chair are perfect places to rest drinks or books.

A. Cut the arms **(G)** to size.

B. For decoration, cut a triangle with 1½"-long sides from the front corners of each arm, using a jigsaw or circular saw (photo left).

C. Make a tapered cut on the inside, back edge of each arm. Mark points for the cut onto the back end of each arm, 3¼" in from each inside edge. Mark the outside edges 10" from the back, connect the points, then cut the tapers with a circular saw or jigsaw.

D. Sand all edges smooth.

6 **Assemble the arms, cleats and posts.** The arms are supported by posts in front, and a cleat that is attached to the backs of the chair slats.

A. Cut the arm cleat **(F)** and make a mark 2½" in from each end.

B. Set the cleat on edge on your worksurface. Position the arms on the top edge of the cleat so the back ends of the arms are flush with the back of the cleat and the untapered edge of each arm is aligned with the 2½" mark.

C. Fasten the arms to the cleats using glue and counterbored 3" deck screws.

D. Cut the posts **(H)** to size, then use a compass to mark a 1¾"-radius roundover cut on each bottom post corner (the rounded bottoms make the Muskoka chair more stable on uneven surfaces).

E. Position the arms on top of the square ends of the posts, with the faces of the post parallel to the sides of the arms. The posts should be set back 1½" from the front ends of the arm, and 1" from the inside edge of the arm.

F. Fasten the arms to the posts with glue and counterbored 3" deck screws (photo below).

G. Cut tapered arm braces (I) from wood scraps, making sure the grain of the wood runs lengthwise.

H. Position an arm brace at the outside of each arm/post joint, centred side to side on the post.

I. Attach each brace with glue and 2" counterbored deck screws driven through the inside face of the post and into the brace, near the top (photo above right).

J. Drive a 2" deck screw down through each arm and into the top of the brace.

Drive screws through each post and into the top of an arm brace to stabilize the arm/post joint.

7 **Assemble the chair.** All that remains to complete the construction of the Muskoka chair is joining the back, seat/leg assembly and arm/post assembly. Before you start, gather up some scrap pieces of wood to use to help brace the parts while you fasten them together.

A. Set the seat/leg assembly onto your worksurface, clamping a piece of scrap wood to the front apron to raise the front of the assembly until the bottoms of the legs are flush on the surface (about 10").

B. Use a similar technique to brace the arm/post assembly so the bottom of the back cleat is 20" above the worksurface.

C. Arrange the arm/post assembly so the posts fit around the front of the seat/leg assembly, with the bottom edge of the

Attach the square ends of the posts to the undersides of the arms, being careful to position the part correctly.

apron flush with the front edges of the posts.

D. Drill a ¼"-dia. pilot hole through the inside of each leg and partway into the post.

E. Drive a ⅜x2½"-long lag screw (with washer) through each pilot hole, but do not tighten completely in case you need to make any assembly adjustments (photo above right).

F. Remove the braces.

G. Slide the back into position so the low back brace is between the legs, and the slats are resting against the front of the arm cleat.

H. Clamp the back to the seat support with a C-clamp, making sure the top of the low brace is flush with the tops of the legs where they meet.

I. Use a square to check that the ends of the seat slats meet the front faces of the back slats at a right angle. If they do not, adjust the relative position of the assemblies until a right angle is achieved.

J. Fully tighten the lag screws at the post/leg joints, then add a second lag screw at each joint.

K. Drive three evenly spaced 1½" deck screws through counterbored pilot holes (near the top edge of the arm cleat) and into back slats to secure back.

L. Drive 3" screws through the legs and into the ends of the lower back brace.

8 Apply finishing touches. Clearcoat cedar or leave it to weather naturally.

A. Glue ¼"-thick, ⅜"-dia. cedar wood plugs into all the visible screw counterbores (photo below right).

B. After the glue dries, sand the plugs level with the surrounding surface.

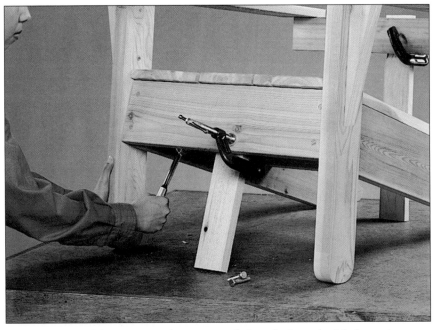

Clamp wood braces to the parts of the chair to hold them in position while you fasten the parts together.

Glue cedar plugs into counterbores to conceal the screw holes.

C. Finish-sand all the exposed surfaces with 120-grit sandpaper.

D. Finish as desired – we simply applied a coat of clear wood sealer.

YARD & GARDEN CART

You can haul bushels of work with this versatile and attractive cart, and carry your long-handled tools, too.

Why be satisfied with a plain wheelbarrow when you can build this beautiful and functional yard-and-garden cart. You will find the long handle (which flips down to create a stand for holding the cart upright) makes moving heavy loads much easier, and the notches in the top rail will keep your long-handled tools from falling out. You can build this out of cedar for a natural look or out of pine and paint it to match other garden tools.

OVERALL SIZE:
28½ " HIGH
31" WIDE
72" LONG

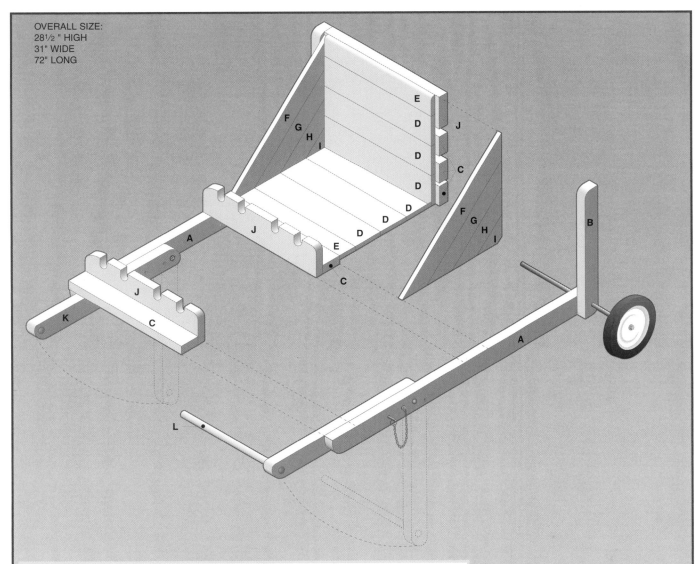

Cutting List

Key	Part	Dimension	Pcs.	Material
A	Back support	1½ x 3½ x 57"	2	Cedar
B	Front support	1½ x 3½ x 23½"	2	Cedar
C	Cross rail	1½ x 3½ x 24"	5	Cedar
D	Bin slat	⅞ x 5½ x 22¼"	6	Cedar
E	End slat	⅞ x 3½ x 22¼"	2	Cedar
F	Bin side	⅞ x 3½ x 28"	2	Cedar
G	Bin side	⅞ x 3½ x 21"	2	Cedar
H	Bin side	⅞ x 3½ x 14"	2	Cedar
I	Bin side	⅞ x 3½ x 7"	2	Cedar
J	Top rail	1½ x 5½ x 24"	3	Cedar
K	Arm	1½ x 3½ x 32"	2	Cedar
L	Handle	1"-dia. x 21"	1	Dowel

Note: Measurements reflect the actual size of dimensional lumber.
Materials: Deck screws (2", 2½"), 4d finish nails (2), 10" utility wheels (2), steel axle rod (30"), ³⁄₁₆"-dia. cotter pins, ⅜"-dia. hitch pins and chain (2), ⅜x4" carriage bolts (2) with locknuts and washers, sandpaper, paint or sealer.

Construction Materials

Qty.	Lumber
1	2x6" x 8' cedar
5	2x4" x 8' cedar
2	1x6" x 8' cedar
2	1x4" x 8' cedar
1	1"-dia.x3' dowel

Test with a square *to make sure the front sup-ports and back supports are joined at right angles.*

Directions: Yard & Garden Cart

1 **Build the cart frame.** The frame of the cart consists of a pair of L-shaped 2x4 assemblies joined together by rails.
A. Cut the back supports **(A)**, front sup-ports **(B)**, three cross rails **(C)** and one of the top rails **(J)**.
B. Use a compass to draw a curve with a 3½" radius on each end of the back sup-ports and on one end of each front sup-port. When the curves are cut, the ends of these parts will have one rounded corner and one square corner.
C. Cut the curves with a jigsaw and sand out any rough spots or saw marks.
D. Position the top rail between the tops of the front supports (the ends that are square at both corners).
E. Fasten the rail between the supports with glue and 2½" deck screws driven through pilot holes (countersink all pilot holes in this project so the screw heads are recessed).
F. Position two cross rails between the front supports, 9" and 14" down from the tops of the front supports.
G. Make sure the cross rails are aligned with the top rail, and attach them with glue and deck screws.
H. Fasten another cross rail between the bottom ends of the front supports; the bottom edge of the cross rail is 3½" up from the bottoms of the front supports and aligned with the other rails.
I. Glue and screw the front supports to the

back supports, using a square to make sure the parts are joined at right angles (photo above). The unshaped ends of the back supports should be flush with the front and bottom edges of the front supports, and the back supports should be attached to the inside faces of the front supports.
J. Drill centred, ½"-dia. holes for the wheel axles through the bottoms of the front supports and back supports, 1¾" in from the inside corner where the front and back supports are joined.

2 **Cut the notched top rails.** Make certain the notch size will fit your tools.
A. Cut the two remaining top rails **(J)**.
B. These rails contain notches that are aligned to create a rack for tool handles. Before cutting the tool notches into the rails, use a compass to draw 1½"-radius roundover curves at each end along one side of each rail.

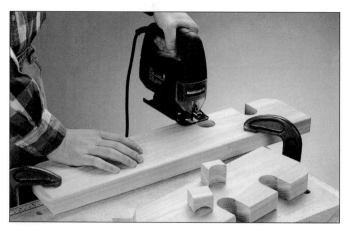

Make straight cuts *from the edge of each rail to the sides of the holes to make the tool notches.*

C. Cut the roundovers with a jigsaw.

D. To make the tool notches in the top rails, draw a reference line 1½" in from the rail edge between the roundovers.

E. Mark four drilling points on the line, 3¾" and 8¼" in from each end.

F. Use a drill and a spade bit to drill 1½"-dia. holes through the drilling points on each rail.

G. Use a square to draw cutting lines from the sides of the holes to the near edge of each rail.

H. Cut along the lines with a jigsaw to complete the tool notches (photo opposite page bottom).

3 **Attach rails between the back supports.** This forms the sturdy frame.

A. Cut two cross rails (C) and lay them flat on your worksurface.

B. Attach a top rail to the edges of each cross rail, so the ends are flush and the edges of the top rails with the tool notches are facing up.

C. Use 2½" deck screws driven at 4" intervals through the top rails and into the edges of the cross rails.

D. Set one of the assemblies on the free ends of the back supports, flush with the edges. The free edge of the cross rail should be flush with the ends of the back supports.

E. Attach the cross rail with deck screws driven down into the back support.

F. Attach the other rail assembly to the top edges of the back supports so the top rail faces the other rail assembly, and the free edge of the cross rail is 21" from the front ends of the back supports.

4 **Attach the bin slats.** The bin portion of the yard-and-garden cart is formed by cedar slats that are attached to the cart frame.

A. Cut the bin slats (D) and end slats (E) to size.

B. Position one end slat and three bin slats between the front supports, with the end slat flush with the edge of the front cross rail and the last bin slat butted against the back supports. There should be a ⅞" gap between each end of each slat and the front supports.

C. Attach the slats with glue and 2" deck screws driven down through the slats and into the cross rails (photo below).

D. Fasten the rest of the bin slats to the top edges of the back supports, with a ⅞" recess at each end. Start with the slat that fits at the bottom of the bin, and work your way up, driving screws down into the tops of the back supports.

TIP:
Cut pieces of sheet aluminum or galvanized metal to line the cart bin for easy cleaning after hauling. Simply use aviator snips to cut the pieces to fit inside the bin, then attach them with special roofing nails that have rubber gaskets under the nail heads. Make sure that no sharp metal edges are sticking out from the bin.

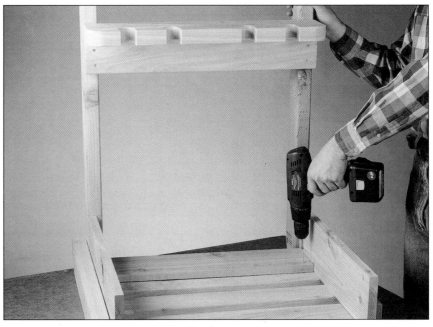

Attach the bin slats *to the front supports, leaving a ⅞"-wide gap at both ends of each slat.*

Round over the tips of the front supports and the front edge of the end slat, using a belt sander.

Fasten the bin sides in a V-shape with glue and deck screws.

E. Fasten the final end slat so it fits between the last bin slat and the lower cross rail on the back supports.

F. Use a belt sander with a coarse belt to round over the front edges of the front end slat and front supports (photo above left).

5 Attach the bin sides. The bin sides fill in the V-shape between the front and back supports. They fit into the recess created between the bin slats and the front supports.

A. Square-cut the bin sides **(F, G, H, I)** to the lengths shown in the Cutting List on page 45.

B. Draw a mitre-cutting line at each end of each bin side.

C. Make the mitre cuts with a mitre box and saw, a circular saw and straightedge, or with a power mitre saw.

D. Fit the short, V-shaped sides into the openings at the sides of the bin, and attach them to the front supports with 2" deck screws.

E. Install the rest of the bin sides in the correct order (photo above right).

6 Make the arms. The arms **(K)** serve a double purpose. First, they support the handles when you wheel the cart. Second, they drop down and lock in place to support the cart in an upright position.

A. Cut the arms to length.

B. Mark the centre of each end of each arm, measuring from side to side.

C. Measure down 3½" from each centre-point, and mark a point.

D. Set the point of a compass at each of these points, and draw a 1¾"-radius semi-circle at each end of both arms.

E. Cut the curves with a jigsaw.

F. Drill a 1"-dia. hole for the handle dowel at one of the centrepoints on each arm.

G. At the other centrepoint, drill a ⅜"-dia. guide hole for a carriage bolt.

7 Attach the arms. The arms are attached with carriage bolts to the back supports.

A. Drill ⅜"-dia. holes for carriage bolts through each back support, 19" from the handle end, and centred between the top and bottom edges of the supports.

B. Insert a ⅜"-dia. x 4"-long carriage bolt through the outside of each ⅜"-dia. hole in the back supports.

C. Slip a washer over each bolt, then slip the arms over the carriage bolts.

D. Slip another washer over the end of each bolt, then secure the arms to the supports by tightening a lock nut onto each bolt. Do not overtighten the lock nut – the arms need to be loose enough that they can pivot freely.

E. Cut the handle **(L)** to length from a 1"-dia. dowel (preferably hardwood).

F. Slide it into the 1"-dia. holes in the ends of the arms.

Drill a pilot hole through each arm and into the ends of the handle, then drive a 4d finish nail into the hole to secure the handle.

G. Secure the handle by drilling pilot holes for 4d finish nails through each arm and into the dowel (photo above), then driving a finish nail into the dowel at each end.

8 Attach the wheels. The wheels for the cart are 10"-dia. utility wheels fitted over a steel axle rod and locked in place with cotter pins. Make sure to buy an axle rod that fits the holes in the hubs of the wheels.

A. Cut the axle rod to 30" in length with a hacksaw, and deburr it with a file or a bench grinder. (Rough-grit sandpaper will also work, but it takes longer and is hard on the hands.)

Secure the wheels by inserting a cotter pin into a hole at the end of each axle, then bending down the arms of the pin with pliers.

B. Secure the axle rod in a vise, or clamp it to your work surface, and use a steel twist bit to drill a 3/16"-dia. hole 1/8" in from each end of the axle.

C. Slip the the axle through the 1/2"-dia. holes drilled at the joints between the front and back supports, then slide two washers over the ends of the axles.

D. Slip a wheel over each axle, add two washers, then insert a 3/16"-dia. cotter pin into each of the holes drilled at the ends of the axle.

E. Secure the wheels by bending down the ends of the cotter pins with a pair of pliers (photo below left).

9 Lock the arms in place. Position this carefully so the cart will stand upright.

A. On a flat surface, fold down the arm/handle assembly so the arms are perpendicular to the ground.

B. Drill a 3/8"-dia. guide hole through each back support, 1" below the carriage bolt that attaches the arms to the supports.

C. Extend the holes all the way through the arms.

D. Insert a 3/8"-dia. hitch pin (or hinge pins will do) into each hole to secure the arms.

E. To prevent losing the pins when you remove them, attach them to the back supports with a chain or a piece of cord.

F. Remove the pins and lift the arms up so they are level with the tops of the back supports.

G. Drill 3/8"-dia. holes through the arms and back supports, about 12" behind the first pin holes, for locking the arms in the cart-pushing position.

10 Apply finishing touches. If you like the natural cedar color, use a clear coat sealer.

A. Smooth out all the sharp edges on the cart with a sander.

B. Sand the surfaces slightly.

C. Apply two coats of exterior wood stain to the wood for protection.

D. Squirt some penetrating/lubricating oil or Teflon® lubricant onto the axles on each side of each wheel to reduce friction.

GARDENER'S TOOLBOX

RECOMMENDED POWER TOOLS

MASTERCRAFT
CIRCULAR SAW

MASTERCRAFT
POWER DRILL

MASTERCRAFT
JIGSAW

MASTERCRAFT
PALM SANDER

RECOMMENDED HAND TOOLS

MASTERCRAFT
BASIC HAND TOOLS

This pleasing and practical accessory will enhance your gardening time.

Make your precious time outdoors more efficient with this handy and attractive toolbox designed specifically for the gardening enthusiast. Special compartments organize seed packages, supplies and hand tools. The bottom shelf will hold a kneeling pad or towels. The handle has a comfortable handgrip cutout and the cedar will withstand moisture and not deteriorate.

Many seeds, soil additives and other common gardening supplies should not be stored outdoors in freezing weather. If you live in a colder climate, load up the toolbox with these items and store it in a warm spot throughout the winter.

Construction Materials

Qty.	Lumber
1	1 x 10" x 6' cedar
1	1 x 6" x 6' cedar
1	1 x 4" x 6' cedar
1	1 x 2" x 6' cedar

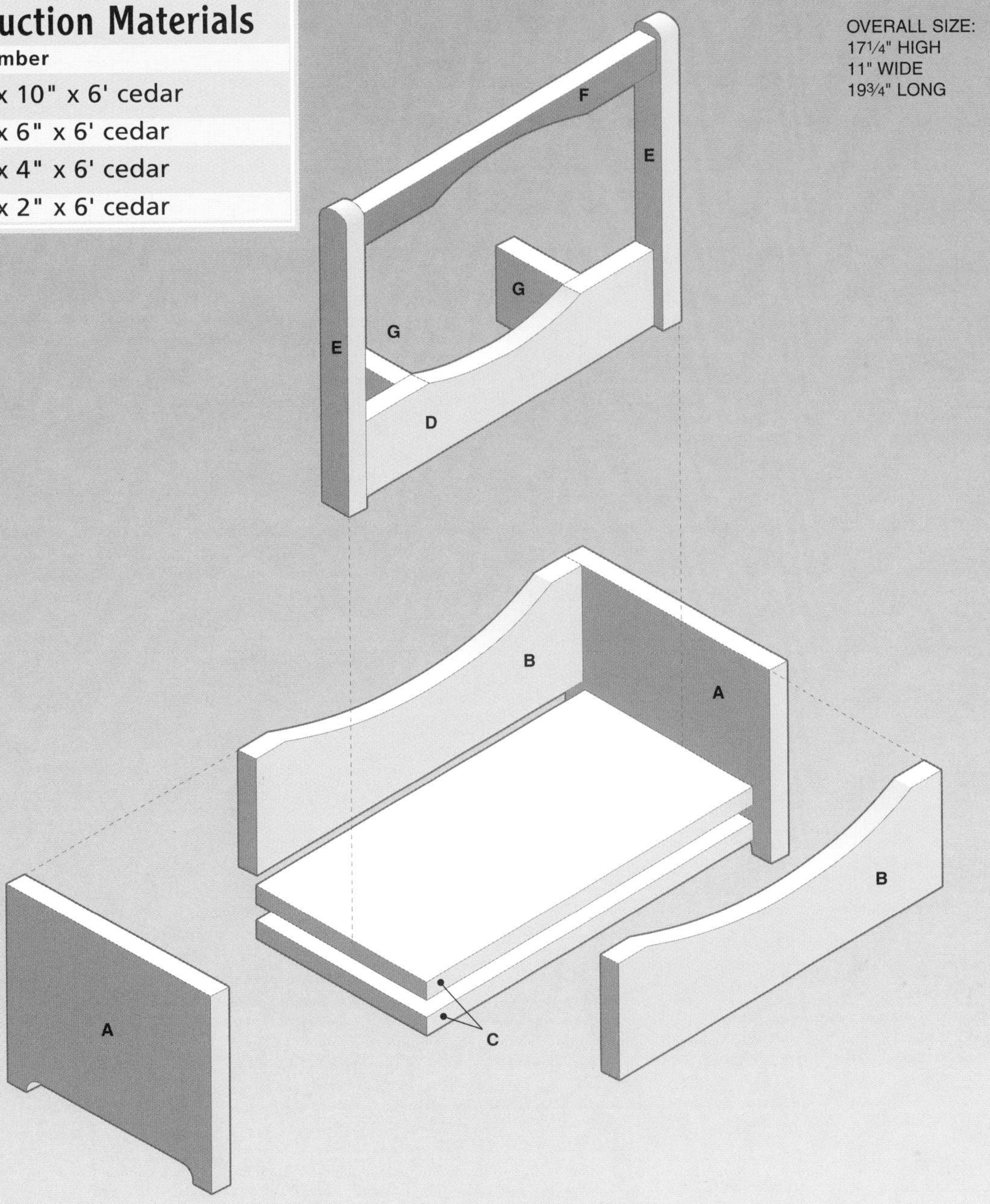

OVERALL SIZE:
17¼" HIGH
11" WIDE
19¾" LONG

Cutting List

Key	Part	Dimension	Pcs.	Material
A	End	⅞ x 9¼ x 11"	2	Cedar
B	Side	⅞ x 5½ x 18"	2	Cedar
C	Shelf	⅞ x 9¼ x 18"	2	Cedar
D	Divider	⅞ x 3½ x 16¼"	1	Cedar
E	Post	⅞ x 1½ x 14"	2	Cedar
F	Handle	⅞ x 1½ x 16¼"	1	Cedar
G	Partition	⅞ x 3½ x 3⅞"	2	Cedar

Note: Measurements reflect the actual size of dimensional lumber.
Materials: Moisture-resistant glue, deck screws (1½", 2"), sandpaper, exterior wood sealer.

Directions: Gardener's Toolbox

1 Build the box. The gardener's toolbox is essentially a wooden box with a handle and a storage shelf beneath the bottom of the box. The sides of the box have curved cutouts to improve access, and the ends have scalloped cutouts to create feet, making the toolbox more stable.

A. Cut the ends **(A)**, sides **(B)** and shelves **(C)** to size.

B. Sand all parts with medium-grit sandpaper to smooth out any rough edges after cutting.

C. On one side, mark points on one long edge, ½" in from the ends. Mark another point, ½" down from the centre of the same long edge.

D. Draw a graceful curve connecting those points, forming the cutting line for the curve at the top.

E. Cut the curve with a jigsaw, and sand it to remove any rough spots.

F. Position this completed side piece on the uncut side piece, so their edges and ends are flush.

G. Trace the curve onto the uncut side, and cut that side piece to match the first.

H. Clamp the sides together, and gang-sand both curves to smooth out any rough spots.

I. To cut the curves on the bottom edges of the ends, first use a compass to draw ¾"-radius semicircles, 1" from each end. These semicircles form the rounded end of each scalloped cutout.

J. Using a straightedge, draw a straight line

Use a jigsaw to cut the curves on the bottom edge of each end, forming feet for the box.

connecting the tops of the circles, completing the cutout shape.

K. Cut the curves with a jigsaw (photo above) and sand the ends to remove any saw marks or other rough spots.

L. To attach the ends to the sides, drill pilot holes for countersunk 2" deck screws at each end, 7/16" in from the edges. Position the pilot holes 1", 3" and 5" down from the tops of the ends.

M. Apply glue to the ends of the sides, and fasten them to the ends with 2" deck screws, driven through the ends and into the sides.

N. Make sure the top and outside edges are flush. Mark the shelf locations on the inside faces of the ends; the bottom of the lower shelf is ¾" up from the bottoms of the ends, and the upper shelf position is 3¾" up from the bottoms of the ends.

O. Drill pilot holes for 2" deck screws 7/16" up from the lines.

P. Apply glue to the shelf ends, and position them between the ends with their bottom edges on the lines.

Q. Drive 2" deck screws through the ends and into the shelves (photo left) to attach the parts.

2 Build the divider assembly. The internal sections of the toolbox are made as a separate assembly and then inserted into the box.

A. Cut the divider **(D)**, posts **(E)**, handle **(F)** and partitions **(G)** to size.

B. Use a sander or a jigsaw to make a 3/8" roundover on the corners of one end of each post.

Attach the shelves by driving deck screws through the ends and into the shelf ends.

Drill countersunk pilot holes through the posts before you attach them to the handle.

C. The divider and handle have shallow arcs cut on one long edge. Draw the arcs on the handle and divider. First, mark points 4" in from each end; then, mark a centred point, 5/8" up from one long edge on the handle. On the divider, mark a centred point 5/8" down from one long edge. Draw a graceful curve to connect the points, and cut along the cutting lines with a jigsaw.

D. Sand all the edges of handle and divider.

E. Drill two countersunk pilot holes on the divider to attach the partitions. Centre the pilot holes 7/16" to each side of the curve.

F. Use moisture-resistant glue and 2" deck screws, driven through the divider and into the partition edges, to attach the partitions to the divider.

G. Clamp the posts together with their ends flush, and mark a 3½"-long reference line on each post, 7/8" in from the joint formed when the parts are clamped together – start the reference lines at the straight post ends. Connect the lines at the tops to indicate the position of the divider ends.

H. Drill two countersunk pilot holes through the posts, centred between each reference line and the inside edge (photo above).

I. Drill two countersunk pilot holes in each post, centred ½" and 1" down from the top ends.

J. Position the divider between the posts, aligned with the pilot holes. One face of the divider should be flush with a post edge.

K. Fasten the handle and divider between the posts with moisture-resistant glue and 2" deck screws.

L. Set the assembly into the box to make sure it fits.

3 **Install the divider.** Use a combination square to make sure handle assembly is perpendicular to the ends.

A. Make sure the partitions fit squarely against the sides.

B. Trace post position lines on the ends (photo below).

C. Apply glue to the ends where the posts will be fastened.

D. Attach the posts to the ends with countersunk 1½" deck screws, driven through the posts and into the ends.

E. Drive two evenly spaced countersunk 2" deck screws through the sides and into each outside partition edge.

4 **Apply the finishing touches.** If you want to preserve the cedar tones, apply clear exterior wood sealer to all the surfaces of the gardener's toolbox. But you may prefer to simply leave the wood uncoated for a more rustic appearance: As you use the toolbox, it will slowly turn grey.

A. Sand all the surfaces with medium (100- or 120-grit) sandpaper to smooth out any rough spots, then finish-sand with fine (150- or 180-grit) sandpaper.

B. Apply finish of choice and let dry thoroughly before use.

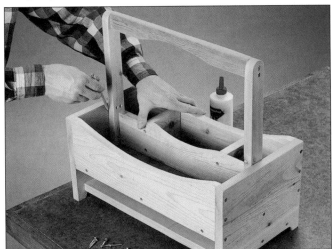

Draw reference lines for the post position on the box ends.

BIRD FEEDER

RECOMMENDED POWER TOOLS

MASTERCRAFT

CIRCULAR SAW

MASTERCRAFT

POWER DRILL

MASTERCRAFT

JIGSAW

MASTERCRAFT

PALM SANDER

• glue gun

RECOMMENDED HAND TOOLS

MASTERCRAFT

BASIC HAND TOOLS

This simple and functional feeder can be built in an afternoon, mostly from scrap materials.

While you can build this bird feeder out of other materials, the cedar lap siding used here is ideal. Cedar withstands deterioration caused by the weather for many years, even without sealing or painting. The tapered profile of the siding creates a pleasing look for the feeder, particularly on the roof. You probably have the rest of the necessary materials left over from other projects, making this a very inexpensive project to build. (If you have some siding left over, you only need about 6½', but you usually can't buy less than a 10' length.)

To fill this cleverly designed feeder, simply turn the threaded rod so that the hook is aligned with the slot in the roof. Lift up the roof, fill the box with bird food, replace the roof and turn the rod to lock the roof back in place.

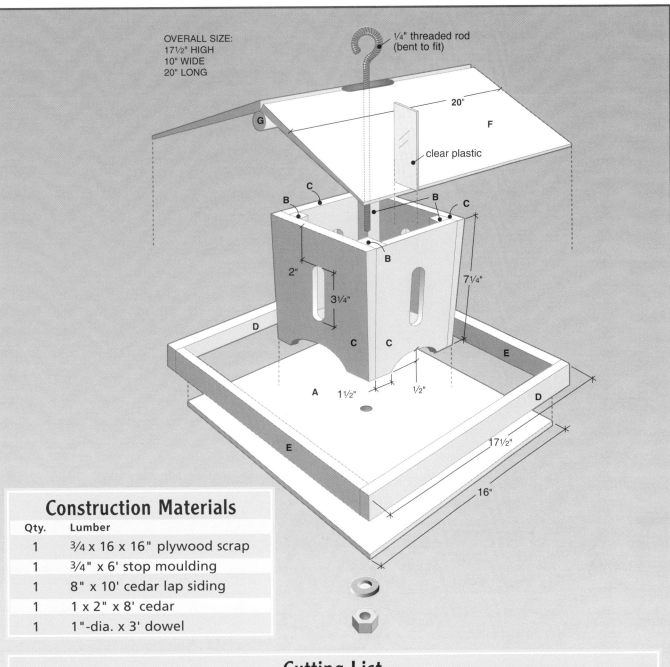

OVERALL SIZE:
17½" HIGH
10" WIDE
20" LONG

¼" threaded rod
(bent to fit)

20"

F

clear plastic

G

B
C
C
B
B

2"
3¼"
7¼"

D

C
C

E

A
1½"
½"

D

E

17½"

16"

Construction Materials

Qty.	Lumber
1	¾ x 16 x 16" plywood scrap
1	¾" x 6' stop moulding
1	8" x 10' cedar lap siding
1	1 x 2" x 8' cedar
1	1"-dia. x 3' dowel

Cutting List

Key	Part	Dimension	Pcs.	Material
A	Base	¾ x 16 x 16"	1	Plywood
B	Post	¾ x ¾ x 7¼"	4	Cedar
C	Box side	5/16 x 6 x 7¼"	4	Cedar siding
D	Ledge side	¾ x 1½ x 17½"	2	Cedar
E	Ledge end	¾ x 1½ x 16"	2	Cedar
F	Roof panel	5/16 x 7¼ x 20"	2	Cedar siding
G	Ridge pole	1"-dia. x 20"	1	Dowel

Note: Measurements reflect the actual size of dimensional lumber.
Materials: ¼"-dia. threaded, galvanized or brass rod with matching nut and washer, wood glue, hot-melt glue, 4d common nails, rigid acrylic or plastic.

Directions: Bird Feeder

1 **Cut and prepare the base.** A scrap of exterior grade plywood will work best.

A. Cut the plywood base **(A)** from ¾"-thick plywood.

B. Draw straight diagonal lines from corner to corner to locate centre of square base.

C. Measure and mark a 6" square in the middle of the base, making sure the lines are parallel to the edges of the base. This square shows the eventual location of the feeder box.

D. Drill a ¼"-dia. hole through the centre of the base where the lines cross.

E. Measure in towards centre ⅜" from each corner of the 6" square and mark points.

F. Drill 1/16"-dia. pilot holes all the way through the base at these points (photo below).

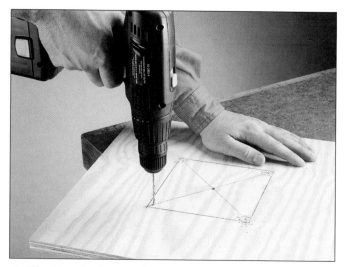

Drill pilot holes *at the corners of the feeder box location that is laid out on the plywood base.*

2 **Prepare the feeder box parts.** The posts and box sides form the walls of the feeder box. Vertical grooves in the box sides create viewing windows so you can check the food level. Small arcs cut in the bottoms of box sides control the flow of food through to the feeding area.

A. Cut the posts **(B)** to size from ¾"-square cedar stop moulding (if you prefer, you can rip a 3'-long piece of ¾"-thick cedar to ¾" in width to make the posts).

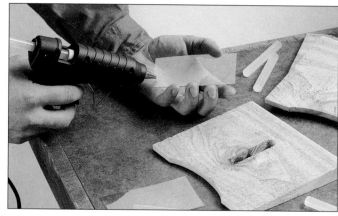

Cover the viewing slots *by hot-gluing clear plastic or acrylic pieces to the inside face of each panel.*

B. From 8" cedar lap siding (actual dimension is 7¼") cut two 6"-wide box sides **(C)**.

C. Cut two more panels to about 7" in width; these will be trimmed to follow the lap-siding bevels.

D. Cut a viewing slot in each box side. First, drill two ½"-dia. starter holes for a jigsaw blade along the centre of each box side – make one hole 2" from the top, and the other 2" from the bottom.

E. Connect the starter holes by cutting with a jigsaw to cut the slots.

F. Cut a ½"-deep arc into the bottom of each box side, using the jigsaw. Start the cuts 1½" from each end.

G. Smooth out the arcs with a drum sander mounted on a power drill.

H. Cut strips of clear acrylic or plastic slightly larger than the viewing slots.

I. Hot-glue the strips behind the slots on the inside faces of the box sides (photo above).

J. To mark cutting lines for trimming two box sides to follow the siding bevel, tape box side together into a box shape. Wide ends of bevelled siding should all be flush.

K. Trace the siding profile onto the inside faces of the two box ends.

L. Disassemble box. Cut along profile lines with a jigsaw.

3 **Assemble the feeder box.** Make sure you keep the feeder box square as the glue dries.

A. Wood glue the posts flush with the inside edges on the box sides that are trimmed to follow the bevel profile. Clamp until dry.

Insert spacers 2" in from the "eaves" of the roof to set the pitch before applying glue to the seam.

B. Complete the assembly by gluing the untrimmed box sides to the posts. Clamp until dry.

4 **Install the base frame.** You may want to seal the edges of the base before attaching frame.

A. Cut the ledge sides **(D)** and ledge ends **(E)** from 1x2 cedar, to build a frame around base so bird food does not spill out.

B. Glue and attach ledge pieces so bottoms are flush with the bottom of the base.

C. Reinforce the joint with 4d common nails.

5 **Attach the base.** A spacer will help you align the box square to the base.

A. Align the assembled feeder box with the 6" square drawn on the base.

B. Glue the box to the base on these lines, then turn the entire assembly upside down.

C. Attach the base to the feeder box by driving 4d galvanized common nails through the pre-drilled pilot holes in the base and into the posts on the feeder box.

6 **Make the roof.** An extra set of hands may be helpful here.

A. Cut ridge pole **(G)** from a 1"-dia. dowel.

B. Cut the roof panels **(F)** from 8" siding.

C. Lay the panels on your worksurface so the wide ends butt together.

D. Slip a 1"-thick spacer 2" in from each of the narrow ends to create the roof pitch.

E. Apply a heavy bead of hot glue into the seam between panels (photo above), then quickly press the ridge pole into the seam before the glue hardens completely.

F. Let glue harden for at least 15 minutes.

G. Set roof down (right-side-up) so the ends of the ridge pole each rest on a 2x4 block.

H. Drill ⅜"-dia. holes through the roof and the ridge pole, 1" on each side of the midpoint of the ridge.

I. Use a jigsaw to connect the two holes, cutting on both sides of the holes to create a 2"-long slot.

J. Cut the ¼"-dia. threaded rod to 16" in length, then use pliers to bend a 1½"-dia. loop in one end of the rod.

K. Thread the unbent end of the rod through the slot in the roof and the hole in the base (photo below), then spin the rod loop so it is perpendicular to the roof ridge (preventing it from slipping into the slot).

L. Tighten a washer and nut onto the end of the rod, loosely enough that the loop can be spun with moderate effort.

7 **Finishing touches.** Left untreated, the wood will weather to a silver-grey colour.

A. Sand surfaces smooth.

B. Apply the finish you desire; paint or a wood sealer works well. Make sure the finish is not toxic to birds – we did not apply a finish to our bird feeder.

The bird feeder is held together by a looped, threaded rod that runs through the roof and is secured with a washer and nut on the underside of the base.

BIKE RACK

RECOMMENDED POWER TOOLS

MASTERCRAFT
CIRCULAR SAW

MASTERCRAFT
POWER DRILL

MASTERCRAFT
JIGSAW

MASTERCRAFT
PALM SANDER

- belt sander or belt/disc sander

RECOMMENDED HAND TOOLS

MASTERCRAFT
BASIC HAND TOOLS

This clever storage rack safely stores your family bikes, biking tools and supplies.

This versatile bicycle rack stores two adult-size bikes and two children's bikes out of the way. It also features two handy storage compartments at the base where you can organize bicycle tools, spare inner tubes and other accessories so you always know where they are. The sliding racks that hold the bikes are padded to protect the paint on the bike frames. You even can do maintenance work on the bikes while they are secured in the racks. If you need to hold four adult-size bikes in the rack, just make the rack posts taller.

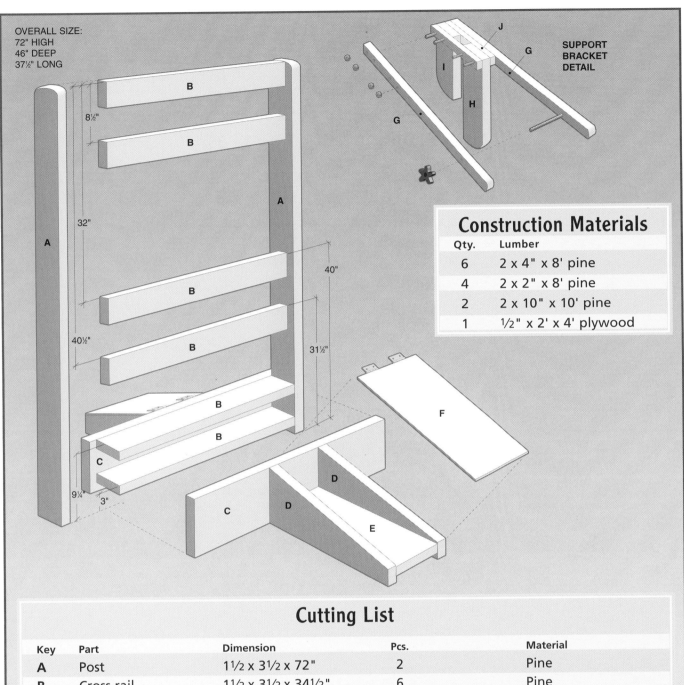

OVERALL SIZE:
72" HIGH
46" DEEP
37½" LONG

SUPPORT
BRACKET
DETAIL

Construction Materials

Qty.	Lumber
6	2 x 4" x 8' pine
4	2 x 2" x 8' pine
2	2 x 10" x 10' pine
1	½" x 2' x 4' plywood

Cutting List

Key	Part	Dimension	Pcs.	Material
A	Post	1½ x 3½ x 72"	2	Pine
B	Cross rail	1½ x 3½ x 34½"	6	Pine
C	Cross brace	1½ x 9¼ x 37½"	2	Pine
D	Foot	1½ x 9¼ x 19¾"	4	Pine
E	Foot base	1½ x 9¼ x 19¾"	2	Pine
F	Cover	½ x 12¼ x 21"	2	Plywood
G	Bracket arm	1½ x 1½ x 20"	16	Pine
H	Bracket leg	1½ x 3½ x 13½"	8	Pine
I	Bracket leg	1½ x 3½ x 6½"	8	Pine
J	Bracket spacer	½ x 1½ x 8½"	16	Plywood

Note: Measurements reflect the actual size of dimensional lumber.
Materials: Glue, wood screws (#8 x 2½", #8 x 3"), ⅜"-dia. x 6" carriage bolts (40) with nuts and washers, 16 threads-per-inch ⅜"-dia. plastic knobs (8), 1½ x 1½" utility hinges (4), closed-cell foam strips, sandpaper, polyurethane or paint, wax.

Directions: Family Bike Rack

1 **Build the main frame.** The main frame of this bike rack consists of two 6'-tall posts that support pairs of 2x4 cross rails. When the rack is completed, the upper pairs of rails will hold the brackets that support the bikes.

A. Cut the posts **(A)** to length, then round off the top ends with a jigsaw and sand the curves smooth (a belt or belt/disc sander mounted on its side to your worksurface can be used to make the roundovers).

B. Draw a centreline from top to bottom on the inside face of each post to use as a reference for positioning the cross rails.

C. Cut the cross rails **(B)** and attach them between the posts with glue and #8x3" wood screws. The top four cross rails should be centred on the centrelines, with their broad faces pointing out.

D. Attach the top rail flush with the tops of the posts; attach the second rail with its top edge 8½" down from the tops of the

Use a circular saw to cut the tapered sides of the feet for the base.

posts; attach the third rail with its top edge 32" down from the tops of the posts; attach the fourth rail with its top edge 40½" down from the tops of the posts.

E. The two rails closest to the bottom should be fastened with broad faces up. Attach them so the tops are 9¼" and 3" up from the bottoms of the posts (photo below left).

2 **Build the base.** The base for this bike rack provides support for the main frame, as well as storage for your tools and equipment. It features two tapered feet that extend out in the front and back of the rack. The feet are attached to heavy 2x10 cross braces that fit around the lower cross rails.

A. Cut the cross braces **(C)**, feet **(D)** and foot bases **(E)** from 2x10 pine.

B. Draw cutting lines for the tapers on the sides of the feet: First mark a point on one end of each foot, 3" up from the bottom corner. Then use a straightedge to draw a line connecting the point with the top corner at the opposite end of the foot.

Attach the bottom pair of cross rails *between the posts with their broad faces up.*

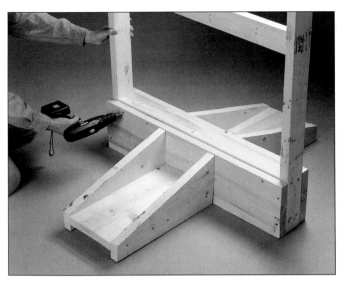

Attach the base assemblies to the posts and bottom cross rails on the main frame.

C. Cut along each cutting line with a circular saw (photo opposite page top).

D. Use glue and #8x3" wood screws to fasten a foot base between each pair of feet, with a 1½" gap between each base and the bottoms of the feet.

E. Attach the foot assemblies to the cross braces, centred from end to end, by driving #8x3" screws through the cross braces and into the ends of the feet.

F. Fasten the assemblies to the main frame by driving screws through the cross braces and into the posts and lower two cross rails (photo above); use glue at all joints, and make sure the ends of the cross braces are flush with the outside faces of the posts.

G. Cut the covers **(F)** for the feet from ½"-thick plywood, and mount them on the cross braces with utility hinges (photo right).

3 **Build support brackets.** The support brackets are essentially wooden clamps that slip over pairs of cross rails and hold the bicycles in place. Two brackets are needed to hold a bicycle: one bracket is clamped to the seat post, and the other to the handlebar post.

A. Cut the bracket arms **(G)**, bracket legs **(H, I)**, and bracket spacers **(J)**.

B. Use a compass set to a 1¾" radius to mark a full roundover on the ends of the taller bracket legs **(H)**.

C. Mark a 1¾" radius on one side only at the ends of the shorter bracket legs **(I)**.

D. Cut off the roundovers on all parts with a jigsaw, then smooth them out on a belt sander mounted to your worksurface.

E. Round over one end of each arm slightly on the belt sander.

F. Place a pair of arms on a flat worksurface so that the square ends are together.

G. Position two spacers between the arms, flush with the square ends.

H. Position one longer bracket leg and one shorter leg between the arms and spacers. The back edge of the shorter leg should be flush with the square ends of the arms (photo following page top left), and the longer leg should be 1½" from the shorter leg (to fit over the 1½"-thick rails). Once you have the pieces in correct position, clamp them together.

I. Drill ⅜"-dia. guide holes for carriage bolts through the arms, spacers and legs (photo following page top left). Space the guide holes for evenly spaced bolts at each leg location.

J. Unclamp the parts, apply glue and fasten the bracket parts together with carriage bolts, washers and nuts.

K. Insert a 2x4 spacer between the free ends of the arms, and drill a ⅜"-dia. hole through both arms, 4" in from the ends of the arms. This hole is for the carriage bolts used to draw the arms together around the bicycle frame.

Attach hinged covers to the cross braces of the base to protect the storage space.

Align the bracket arms, *spacers and bracket legs, then drill 3/8"-dia. guide holes for carriage bolts.*

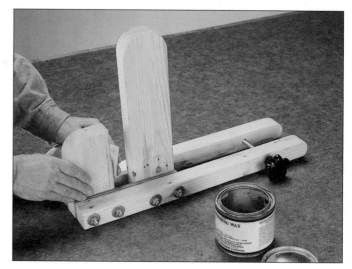

Apply paste wax *to the insides of the bracket legs and to the main-frame rails as a lubricant.*

L. Remove the spacer. Insert a carriage bolt through the arms so the head is tight against the outside face of one arm.

M. Slip a washer over the free end of the carriage bolt, and twist a threaded knob (3/8"-dia.) on the end. By turning the knob, you can draw the arms together (there is enough flex in 2x2 pine to make this happen). Repeat steps for all support brackets.

4 Apply finishing touches. You will need to renew the wax in step C periodically.

A. Sand all surfaces with medium (100- or 120-grit) sandpaper to smooth out rough spots, then finish-sand with fine (150- or 180-grit) sandpaper.

B. Apply a finish to all the surfaces – we used two coats of polyurethane. Glossy enamel paint is also a good choice if you want a more finished appearance.

C. Apply two or three coats of paste wax to cross rails and inside edges of leg braces. Buff each coat until hardened (photo above right). This allows braces to move easier.

D. Cut pieces of thin (3/8"- to 1/2"-thick) closed-cell foam to fit over the ends of the arms on the brackets.

E. Staple the foam onto the ends to protect the bicycle frame (photo right).

F. To use the bike rack, slip pairs of brackets over the top cross rail in each pair in the main frame. The cross rail should fit between the bracket legs.

G. Test each bracket to make sure it is secure, then adjust the positions of the brackets so they align with the seat post and handlebar post of your bike.

H. Lift bike up so posts fit between the ends of the arm pairs in each bracket. Tighten star-shaped knob at ends of each arm pair until posts are held securely between arms.

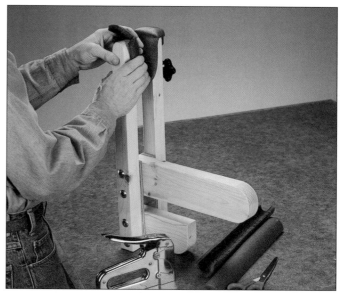

Staple closed-cell foam strips *onto the ends of the bracket arms to protect the bike frame.*